On India

On India

Self-image and Counter-image

Edited by
Anindita N. Balslev

SAGE www.sagepublications.com
Los Angeles • London • New Delhi • Singapore • Washington DC

First published in 2013 by

 SAGE Publications India Pvt Ltd
B1/I-1 Mohan Cooperative Industrial Area
Mathura Road, New Delhi 110 044, India
www.sagepub.in

SAGE Publications Inc
2455 Teller Road
Thousand Oaks, California 91320, USA

SAGE Publications Ltd
1 Oliver's Yard, 55 City Road
London EC1Y 1SP, United Kingdom

SAGE Publications Asia-Pacific Pte Ltd
33 Pekin Street
#02-01 Far East Square
Singapore 048763

Published by Vivek Mehra for SAGE Publications India Pvt Ltd, Phototypeset in 10/13 pt Aldine401 BT by Diligent Typesetter, Delhi and printed at De-Unique, New Delhi.

Library of Congress Cataloging-in-Publication Data

Library of Congress Cataloging-in-Publication Data
On India: self-image and counter-image/edited by Anindita N. Balslev.
    pages cm
  Includes bibliographical references and index.
1. India—History. 2. Self-perception—India. 3. Self-evaluation—India.
I. Balslev, Anindita N.
  DS436.057   954—dc23   2013   2012049737

ISBN: 978-81-321-1092-7 (HB)

The SAGE Team: Neelakshi Chakraborty, Punita Kaur Mann
                and Sanjeev Kumar Sharma

To those for whom cross-cultural conversation is a new way
of learning about what we all must unlearn

Thank you for choosing a SAGE product! If you have any comment, observation or feedback, I would like to personally hear from you. Please write to me at contactceo@sagepub.in

—Vivek Mehra, Managing Director and CEO,
SAGE Publications India Pvt Ltd, New Delhi

Bulk Sales

SAGE India offers special discounts for purchase of books in bulk. We also make available special imprints and excerpts from our books on demand.

For orders and enquiries, write to us at

Marketing Department
SAGE Publications India Pvt Ltd
B1/I-1, Mohan Cooperative Industrial Area
Mathura Road, Post Bag 7
New Delhi 110044, India
E-mail us at marketing@sagepub.in

Get to know more about SAGE, be invited to SAGE events, get on our mailing list. Write today to marketing@sagepub.in

This book is also available as an e-book.

Contents

Foreword

In December 2010, a three-day seminar on 'On India: Self-image and Counter-image' was organized in Delhi by Anindita Balslev on behalf of her forum 'Cross-cultural Conversation'. This was supported by the Indira Gandhi National Centre for the Arts (IGNCA) as well as the Indian Council for Cultural Relations (ICCR). She brought together a wide spectrum of scholars and thinkers from around the world who engaged in an extensive and creative dialogue. The present volume contains a selected number of papers first presented at the CCC Conference and then revised for this significant publication.

India is a pluralistic, multifaceted and many-splendoured civilization and, like a crystal with many facets, also has multiple images. It is amazing that despite a whole series of foreign invasions and disruption for a thousand years, India retains its cultural identity and its democratic polity. How this is looked upon abroad varies with the viewpoint of the author. There is the 'romantic India' of maharajas and snake charmers, there is the negative image of endemic poverty and corruption and in between the image of a modern, vibrant nation growing rapidly with tremendous talent and manpower reserves. Each one of these has an element of truth, and the endeavour in the seminar was to look upon the Indian civilization from many different points of view.

I was unable to attend the inauguration, but in my valedictory speech I highlighted the point that the secret of India's persistence down through the millennia, despite numerous invasions, holocausts and colonialism, was due to some basic civilizational principles that are enshrined in the Upanishads, such as the concept that 'truth is one, the wise call it by many names', *ekam sat vipraha bahudha vadanti*; the realization that the human race is a single family, *vasudhaiva kutumbakam*; the commitment to the welfare of the many, the happiness of the many, *bahaman sukhayaya bahujan hitayata*. The pluralistic multi-ethnic, multi-regional, multi-religious and multilinguistic character of the Indian people have combined to create a unique nation.

The Constitution that we adopted in 1950 after our freedom in 1947 articulates the basic ideals upon which India is based. The ideals of equality, liberty, freedom of the press and the individual, an independent judiciary and special provisions for the backward and least privileged sections of the society have enabled us to workout a vibrant democratic system for over 60 years, while so many former colonial nations in Asia and Africa, despite being independent, still lack democracy.

This 'Cross-cultural Conversation' is the third in a series of conferences held in New Delhi, the first being organized by Dr Anindita Balslev in 2006. I commend her initiative and energy in single-handedly organizing this international conversation. I am sure the contents of this book will be of great interest to students of Indian politics, economics and sociology around the world. It is clear that the human race is willy-nilly moving into a global society which, by definition, will have to be pluralistic and multifaceted. India is thus a vibrant example of the sort of multiculturalism that must ultimately pervade the world. Conversations of this nature can therefore help to create the intellectual foundation for such a society.

1 January 2013

Karan Singh
President
Indian Council for Cultural
Relations
Chairman
Auroville
Chancellor
Benares Hindu University

Preface

Reflections on India today call for a careful scrutiny of a host of different issues that have a bearing not only on our understanding of India's past but also on our collective endeavours and aspirations for tomorrow. Given the wide range of queries regarding this vast subject matter, it is obvious that only a few of these could be addressed within the limited scope of this volume. There is need as well as room for an open ongoing conversation among participants who are truly committed to share their concerns from multiple perspectives, bringing in their respective experience and specialization required for such a project.

It is precisely therefore that this collection of essays *On India: Self-image and Counter-image* is especially significant since these are contributed by persons who have engaged themselves over the years, striving to comprehend the forces that are at work in the Indian cultural soil, influencing the lives of millions. The principal focus of this endeavour is on some 'images' of India that are construed both by insiders and outsiders with respect to the geopolitically bounded space called India. A study of these images can be fruitful in many ways since these tell us the way we perceive ourselves and are being perceived. More importantly, with the influx of new emerging images is the question whether there is a core self-image of India as a persistent feature in the self-understanding of India.

Knowing that there was no dearth of enthusiasm among fellow thinkers—internationally speaking—whose contributions to such an exploratory venture will be valuable, I thought of holding an international conference on the theme of 'India: Self-image and Counter-image' despite the rather limited resource that was available at the time. The hope has been that this way a rich conversation may ensue and multiple voices could be heard on this complex subject. Moreover, it could then inspire the invited participants to rethink on this topic and their contributions might that way turn out to be a bit different than had it been composed prior to any discussion. All these ideas can now be shared with many more readers.

The conference held at the end of December 2010 is the third in a series of cross-cultural conversation (CCC) conferences that have taken place in New Delhi. A brief description of the core aim of the CCC Forum as well as short biographical sketches of the contributors can be read at the end of this volume.

While planning this volume and the conference, it seemed important to keep in mind that the construal of self-image in a wide variety of contexts—be that of nationality or ethnicity, gender or race or of secular and religious matters—does entail overtly or covertly the way we perceive and interpret the 'otherness' of the other. It is noteworthy that in the process of conceptualization and articulation of our collective self-understanding, we do indeed very often draw on the diverse perspectives of this 'otherness' of the other as a point of comparison and contrast. Thus, there arises the need to explore a series of questions. Among these are, to mention a few: How is the self-image of India to be delineated by contrasting it with its counter-image? Are there many images of India or do Indians as well as others coming from outside of India always cherish in their heart of hearts an image of 'Eternal India'? If so, what does the latter entail? How have the travellers visiting this complex cultural soil throughout history perceived and formed images of India? If it is argued that the self-image of India has undergone significant modifications through the different phases of history, it may be asked in what way India's self-image today is construed differently? How does that reflect in various areas of domestic affairs or in foreign policymaking endeavours? Moreover, granted the possibility of contending self-images and counter-images, do the existing stereotypes about the Indian culture—regardless whether these are coming from the quarters of the insiders or outsiders of her geopolitical boundary—call for a fresh assessment? In which ways are the existing paradigms helpful or harmful for obtaining a deeper understanding of India's aspirations for the future?

The essays included in this volume are selected and solicited from among a number of Indian and foreign participants coming from the fields of education, literature, philosophy, history, sociology, Indology, diplomacy, peace research and others who joined this conversation.

Given that the speakers in the CCC Forum are free to express their own concerns and are themselves responsible for the views that they hold, I only reminded them that a few among a range of issues that need to be gradually taken up for discussion within the frame of such endeavours are the following: In what way is India today a continuation of India's past? How does India's modernity reflect the thrust of the idea of 'Eternal India'? How are we to distinguish the concepts of a 'nation' and a 'nation state' as well as the meaning of secularism in the Indian context? What are India's current challenges in social, political or economic terms and which of these should be among the top priorities in domestic and foreign affairs? How is the study of India pursued within and outside of India? Have the established institutional methods and approaches been exclusively to India's advantage? Does a review of how India is studied and perceived in other Asian and Western countries urgently call for a close examination? Many of these have been discussed during the 2010 CCC conference, but of course not all could be included. It can be expected that as the conversation continues, many other queries will gradually be formulated.

As it stands, this collection of essays reflects two major concerns. One is about how cross-cultural conversation focusing on India should proceed today and which are some of the primary issues that need to be urgently addressed. The other is regarding whether India has a core cultural image identifiable among the range of competing images, and if so, how to conceptualize its counter-image when we reimagine India today.

No editorial interference has been made with regard to the way specific contributors have told their stories about self-image or have portrayed the otherness of others, choosing the context or the sources for their own readings.

Beginning with the foreword by Dr Karan Singh, all the essays contained in this volume bring out a range of significant reflections on some of these aforesaid concerns. Johan Galtung discusses what he perceives to be the two faces of India at a time when structural violence is rampant. Balmiki Prasad Singh focuses on what he describes as three images of India. Ashis Nandy makes a critical review of the particular problems of the Indian situation in an age when in contrast to the anticipated decline, religions have re-emerged as a postmodern phenomenon. N. Kazanas focuses on features of India's Vedic tradition, delineating how it has influenced various cultures in the past as well as its status in India today. Shyam Saran looks upon diplomacy as a mode of cross-cultural conversation, assessing its possibilities and limitations. D.R. Kaarthikeyan speaks about how to ensure harmony in a pluralistic society like in India, especially in its multi-religious context. Kapil Kapoor raises a few subtle issues with regard to 'what is given' and 'what is borrowed' as one conceptualizes India today. In his paper, one comes across a retelling of an ancient (Pauranic) self-image which perhaps represents a continuing trend in the self-understanding on the part of many Indians even today. However, he does not omit the critical observations made by Al Beruni with regard to the portrayal of that self-image. Lokesh Chandra probes into what he calls the five propensities dominating Indic thought that have bearing on the Indian way of looking at nature, territory, religion, nature, God and belief in unity in diversity. Sukrita Paul Kumar looks at some Eurocentric constructions while alluding to literature from erstwhile colonial societies of India and Africa. Madhu Kishwar's focus is on the recent shift of India's image as a third world underdeveloped economy to that of a burgeoning economy and how all these affect the situation of the rich and poor in India. Ugo Astuto highlights the images of India that are portrayed in the diaries and chronicles of Italian travellers from Marco Polo onwards.

Indeed, which image among the various contending images—be that of the self or that of the other—is to be regarded as an exaggerated form of glorification or of ignominy often seems to depend on the interpreters. It equally poses a challenge as to whether a common set of values can be eventually recognized across the board to make this sort of interpretive strategies viable and acceptable to all concerned. For example, one notices that within a given discourse, who is described as a terrorist or as a patriot and which course of action is considered to be rational or not largely depends on who the observer is and what he or she stands for. Dietmar Rothermund elaborates how one negotiates compromises in cross-cultural conversation while analyzing such notions as agency, overlapping consensus and other relevant sub-topics. While he observes that "Terrorists are not reasonable persons, they are committed to destruction, even self-destruction", relying on an "uncompromising doctrine" that justifies holy war, Rothermund also takes care to add that not everyone within such a tradition "endorses this particular doctrine and would participate in cross cultural conversations".

Finally, my paper is a response to the question whether there is a core cultural self-image of India. I have discussed a few of the key ideas that have shaped this culture. Reference is made to Vivekananda and Tagore in order to show that no narrow form of nationalistic chauvinism was approved by the leading personalities of India, although there was no lack of patriotism. Indeed, an analysis of the contending strands regarding the notions of patriotism, nationalism and internationalism that are available in the Indian cultural history along with a range of other related questions calls for a continuing conversation.

However, if this collection of essays has succeeded in putting together some of the predominant and even contradictory strands that are present in the historical canvas of India, which readers will find interesting to reflect on, the effort has been worthwhile.

Those who—like myself—have lived in both the hemispheres know that today people everywhere are eager to hear the voices of cosmopolitan thinkers who can show us how to think globally without demolishing local differences and who can fearlessly speak about where lie the conceptual treasures that are specific to a given culture but can benefit all if these are used for that purpose.

A free exploration of ideas and ideals through cross-cultural conversation is crucially important for removing the grotesque asymmetries in the global context. At present, a shared technology is not only making the presence of 'others' more and more glaringly visible, it is also helping us to become aware of a philosophical vacuum in the face of diversity, obliging us to confront the images of 'otherness' of the other critically and honestly. We seem to be in a situation where we are seeking a strong conceptual backing for an authentic pluralism and for devising institutional mechanisms that are urgently required in order to address the contending demands of our time. It seems to me that in the struggle to correct the asymmetries that are present in her own cultural soil, India can benefit by learning from the positive achievements elsewhere. I also believe that it could be immensely fruitful for all concerned if some of the rich conceptual resources of India could be adequately explored and shared with the rest of the world with the view of bridging the gap between the self and the other.

I thank the Indira Gandhi National Centre for the Arts and the Indian Council for Cultural Relations for supporting the CCC International Conference 2010 devoted to the theme 'On India: Self-Image and Counter Image'.

Anindita N. Balslev
New Delhi

1

Is There a Core Cultural Self-image of India?

Anindita N. Balslev

In the face of the tumultuous changes that are taking place in India as elsewhere, the challenge before us is twofold: to recognize fully the specific kind of conceptual struggle at various levels of our collective life that we must engage in as well as to invent and implement institutional mechanisms that can adequately address the demands of our time. A fresh assessment of any given situation and a resolve to gear the changes in a definite direction almost always go hand in hand with re-construing the self and the other, especially by reimagining the self not in sheer abstraction but in relation to the other on a collective front.

The topic of India has now become very trendy and every month we find new books turning up in the market, frequently describing India as a rising superpower, economically as an emerging giant, militarily as gradually getting on par with any advanced nuclear nation, etc. It is not surprising then that the new images of India that are being projected cannot but have bearing on the subtle and critical question about how we are to view ourselves and define our identity today in an intercultural context. Granting these images of prosperity, of political strength and the power of self-defence their due place of importance, especially when viewed in the light of India's recent historical past, a major task before us seems to be able to envision the way all these images can be made subservient to and in harmony with what has been India's own distinct self-image over the centuries. It is precisely in this context, the question that may arise is whether there is really a core cultural image of India cherished in the Indian cultural soil itself (that is, self-image), which still must be deemed worth perpetuating. Apparently that has been largely the view not only of lots of significant insiders but also of many coming from outside the geopolitical boundary of India. Indeed, there seems to be a self-image which we Indians have inherited from time immemorial that has persisted through the vicissitudes of history even when other contending images have vied with each other to take its place. This image of *Sasvata Bharat* (Eternal India), I will argue, is not an expression of any political prudence, not simply an accidental or a later national construal, nor is it crafted by any skilful statesmanship or diplomatic manoeuvre. In brief, this self-image cannot be said to be due to any kind of expediency. If this is to be at all labelled in any way, I am inclined to suggest that it is born of a meta-philosophical insight. Yet, its tantalizing presence seems to have repeatedly persuaded the Indian mind to pay homage to it and to seek to work it out meticulously in every sphere—societal, religious and political alike. As I will cite examples in support of this reading in course of this short chapter, referring to persons and epochs, let this not be taken as an easy way of simply throwing a few big names but as a documentation for watching carefully how that profound self-understanding has been historically at work. Indeed, today it calls for a greater awareness on our part to seize it in its fullness even on a purely conceptual plane to refresh our collective memories with a view to figuring out how best we could make use of this resource as we go about doing each our bit in this multi-ethnic, multi-religious, multilingual place that India is. Or, should we go even further and say that the ramification of this image is so deep that we can extend it to the entire globe for reflection?

Given the complexities of the contemporary situation, it is surely no facile task to seek to capture its deep significance in order to nurture it on the collective plane with the firm intent of translating the idea into action. However, that is not a good enough reason to shirk away from that responsibility and regard it as dispensable. On the contrary, as we struggle to carve out a path through a chaotic and difficult global scenario, it seems more and more that the power of this image has by no means lost its relevance not only for the sake of building a stronger India but also because of the potentialities it has for promoting a more vigorous and flourishing human interrelationship wherever diversity—in its many façades—reigns. In what consists its power and why we must invent the institutional mechanisms to channelize its influence are some of the interconnected questions that we need to seek answers for by repeatedly engaging ourselves in open public conversations. It is noteworthy that more than anything else, this is a message that primarily seeks to bring about an attitudinal change towards the way we perceive ourselves as well as all those whom we call 'others', by resisting such interpretations of diversity as the ones that are proposed by the proponents of any form of radical cultural relativism.

Perhaps it can be argued that the self-image of a culture is itself a cultural construal even when we may never know the story of its making as it surely is in this specific case. As it happens, we can at best go back to the documents belonging to a hoary past that recorded it as it were in an aphoristic style but which has nevertheless reverberated throughout this culture (and also the CCC Conference 2010). In the unfolding of her cultural history, India as the land that stands for this meta-philosophical insight has known several articulations variously expressed in her diverse thought-traditions. It is these oft-cited ancient articulations that hold the innermost self-image of a culture. Take, for example, the statement that is perhaps most often recapitulated: *ekam sat vipra bahudha vadanti* (reality is one, the wise call it by different names). Many philosophies have been raised over the centuries to interpret the content, the insight encapsulated in this statement within the Indian conceptual world itself: Why is it 'One' that is said to underlie all differences? If it is One, why then can it be expressed in various ways and is not simply to be repeated in an unique, monolithic fashion? Why are those who call it by different names, instead of urging that it must always be called by the same name said to be the wise, the learned? As one takes time to go through the story of reflections on each of these questions, one begins to perceive the constituent elements that are ingrained in the composition of that self-image and the impact it has on the culture as a whole. Obviously, I cannot attempt a summary of all these philosophical deliberations here. However, it may be briefly emphasized that among the attempts to explore the idea of reality as one, there emerged a conspicuous understanding of 'oneness' which in sophisticated philosophical jargon has been articulated as non-duality (Advaita).[1] Those acquainted with the philosophy of Advaita know that there are elaborate explanations of why no duality can be predicated of it and why it is ultimately described as inexpressible, at best as that which can be spoken of only in negative terms (*netimukhe*). Reflections show this is not based on empirical observation, it is a transcendental notion.

This is why I am describing India's self-image as being born of a meta-philosophical insight. This has great impact on the construals of the conception of identity—be that religious, national, etc., as cautiously advocated by some of the best minds in this country. Moreover, this self-perception provides conceptual support for the raison d'être of diversity in an astounding way, demonstrating emphatically why diversity cannot be viewed merely as a passing phase but is to be seen as integral to the empirical world, as something which is here to stay rightfully.

The interesting question then is, what is the task of philosophy with regard to these readings and how is that philosophical understanding supposed to actually impact a society? Records show that philosophy can only render the meta-philosophical insight transparent and tell us why any expression of that inexpressible non-duality must identify itself as being one among many such possible expressions. This is obligatory as well on the part of the tradition which is bearer of this insight. Even as we think of this expression in terms of a tradition—cultural, national, religious, etc.—it remains equally mandatory on the part of that tradition to look upon itself as one among many.

Having said that, let us ask what is implied in that reading? All are free to follow the trajectory of their own respective tradition and conceive of their own identity accordingly. This leaves plenty of space for debates and differences but no room for monopoly or of any claim of exclusivity or depiction of the other tradition as false.

Given that some of the broad features of the Advaitic theoretical discourse are quite familiar to a significant number of people, its practical import does not seem to be always adequately appreciated and analyzed. It grants that every tradition has a right to be distinct along with the insistence that it is binding on its part to perceive itself as one among many such traditions and allow others the same space. In other words, this is an attitude that not only validates diversity but also teaches us to respect it. Evidently, what Advaita is in theory, ahimsa is in practice.

Indeed, the subtle consequences of this reading in various contexts have not merely been exposed and amplified in the theoretical discourse, its actual impact—even if not entirely in its full-fledged desirable form—can also be perceived in the unfolding of the cultural life of India. The fact that the Indian cultural soil has been particularly receptive of this view can be seen in the very presence of the members of virtually all different religious traditions in India including those which have originated elsewhere. Its openness to the otherness of the other becomes also evident in offering home to the adherents of those traditions in her own cultural soil who have felt severely persecuted in their own original homelands and were resisting assimilation. Think of the presence of the Parsis since long and more recently of the Tibetans in India. Thus, it is not a call for absorption into the mainstream tradition but rather an openness to diversity that is demonstrated in these cases. It shows that religious or cultural pluralism is not simply supported by an abstract Advaitic discourse or is cherished merely as a theoretical idea but is a view that has greatly influenced attitudes and actual practice of the people. Indeed this is the core image of India—both historically and conceptually. Note in this connection that this is also why secularism in India could be understood in terms of *sarvadharma sambhava*.[2]

However, as we all know, the continued success of such an enterprise in actual practice depends on all the diverse groups who have made their home in this cultural soil and to the extent that this self-image becomes their own as well. One can also think of extending this idea to a global multi-religious context and imagine the far-reaching consequences this will have when implemented. An open public discourse is needed for capturing the subtleties entailed in this self-image in order to overcome the fear of a loss of identity and perceive in it instead the best collective defence for the cause of diversity.

Basically this is an attitude that has not merely provided a mark of cultural identity or image to India, it also enables us to recognize the counter-image that we must shun. We need to gradually explore in what sense this self-image has not only influenced socio-religious thinking but has also provided political visions and inspired social commitments as exemplified in the lives and actions of some of the greatest Indians and why it remains urgent to deal with that legacy today. From a perusal of relevant documents, it truly seems that no matter how notions of patriotism, nationalism in specific epochs were actually shaped differently, loyalty to this self-understanding was hardly betrayed by any of them.

However, prior to going deeper into this question in the Indian context, let us briefly take note of the way that basic outlooks play a crucial role in shaping the responses to diversity which eventually find expression in societal action planning or even in foreign policymaking enterprises. For this, let me refer to that all too well-known essay by Huntington where he observed that despite their differences, a German and an Italian village can be brought under a common European civilizational paradigm but that—to put it in his own words—"Arabs, Chinese and Westerners ... are not part of any broader cultural entity ... they constitute civilizations.... For the relevant future, there will be no universal civilization, but instead a world of different civilizations." Consequently, this leads Huntington to predict a 'clash of civilizations'.

While examining closely this perception, one cannot help but notice that there is a sense of conceptual vacuum, an absence of an alternative philosophical outlook that could have prompted a different way of looking at the global scenario where difference and diversity do not necessarily provoke antagonism towards the otherness of the other, even where there is no need to conceive of an 'universal civilization', especially if by that is meant a point where diversities get underplayed or dissolved.

To me, this only shows how badly we need cross-cultural conversation, be that for noticing the overlaps despite differences or for appreciating the fact that diversity is not only inevitable but can in many ways be a resource. Obviously, there seems to be an attitudinal bias somewhere that only an alternative philosophical approach can correct.

Today while sharing a technological civilization, we are criss-crossing the globe within a short span of time and messages are being conveyed within a matter of seconds, we are frequently hearing political slogans with regard to our 'living in an interdependent world' or in a 'global village'. Notice that this can hardly be said to match that insight which originated in the cultural landscape of India as expressed in the utterance *vasudhaiva kutumbakam*, that is, 'the whole world is a family'. Although the idea of globe as a common marketplace is now in vogue and also embedded in the very notion of globalization, this does not provoke any imagery of a supportive structure as that of a family.

Once again, in the projection of the core self-image of India, there is no preaching of annulment of particularities or specificities of cultural expressions since there is an insistence here to look upon oneself as one among many. What is remarkable is that it is in fact possible to derive regulative principles from such insights in a world which is vitiated by conflicts and violence. Thus, although there is much to be worked out with regard to how this self-image can be made relevant in specific contexts, there is nevertheless historical evidence showing that this philosophy can actually nurture and promote certain values (such as ahimsa) that are central not only to social ethics but can also be applied even in the context of political struggle. Powerful slogans such as 'hate the system, do not hate the people' as coined by Gandhi during the struggle for India's independence is an exemplification of such a change of strategy based on these values.

Nowadays when conflicts emerge in any multi-ethnic, multi-religious and multilingual context even within a national scene, the question of where to lay our ultimate allegiance arises. There seems to be, clearly, a need for a philosophical outlook to guide us in such situations at various levels of exchanges and interactions, especially in countries which are plural in multifarious ways. Those who like to pay attention to the theoretical side of the value-oriented controversies will enjoy a report of such a debate within the context of the United States. Already in 1994 in a much-read and discussed paper published in the *New York Times*, the distinguished American philosopher Richard Rorty was urging the Americans, especially the American Left, not to disdain patriotism as a value and indeed to give central importance to "the emotion of national pride" and "a sense of shared national identity". He argued that the Americans cannot even criticize themselves unless they also "rejoice" in defining themselves in terms of their national identity. Rorty said so because he thought that the primary alternative to a politics based on patriotism and national identity will be what he calls a "politics of difference". By politics of difference is meant the kind of politics which is based on internal divisions among America's ethnic, racial, religious and other subgroups. In the Indian context, one will need to add caste to that list. The proponents of nationalism do not practically seem to make any concession to cosmopolitanism in politics or in education, they argue that loyalty to one's own nationhood is to be regarded as ultimate and that is the only way out.

Martha Nuusbaum, the well-known American philosopher, objected to Rorty's view saying that he "nowhere considers the possibility of a more international basis for political emotion and concern". For her, a politics based on a shared national identity actually ignores what all of us transnationally share as both rational and mutually dependent human beings. She seeks to strengthen her stand drawing support from the writings of Tagore and refers to his famous novel *The Home and the World*.[3]

I agree with Nuusbaum when she writes that

> Tagore sees deeply when he sees that at bottom nationalism and ethnocentric particularism are not alien to one another, but akin — that to give support to nationalist sentiments subverts, ultimately, even the values that hold a nation together, because it substitutes a colorful idol for the substantive universal values of justice and right.

In this connection, it is also worth remembering that the notion of nationhood in the Indian context has already been for quite some time a matter for deliberations specifically with regard to the ways it is different from the nineteenth century European idea of a nation state. It has been debated whether it is more appropriate to describe India as a civilizational state rather than a nation state while drawing various implications therefrom. However, leaving aside these debates for the moment, what is most fascinating is to observe how again and again—even in those charged chaotic scenarios of the very difficult and gruesome days of the struggle for independence—some of the greatest minds of India reflect, whether always consciously or not, their profound allegiance to that self-image.

Take, for example, how Vivekananda, claimed by many to be the father of Indian nationalism, was conceiving nationalism as an idea deeply rooted in some form of internationalism already at the end of the nineteenth century. While taking intense pride in India's cultural legacy at a time of great humiliation and considering it to be his task to remind the Indians that India has her own mission, he utters without any hesitation that

> every nation has a national purpose of its own. Either in obedience to the Law of nature, or by virtue of the superior genius of the great ones, the social manners and customs of every nation are being moulded into shape, so as to bring that purpose to fruition.

He even talked already at that time about emancipation from national egoism while attaining 'Swaraj'.

However, it is crucially important to keep in mind that to have the conceptual resource is not the same as having it fully worked out or as actually achieving it. Far from it. This is precisely why Swami Vivekananda tried hard to make his fellow countrymen perceive that it is not enough to hail Advaita Vedanta only as an abstract philosophical discourse, his mission became to propagate what he called Practical Vedanta. We find him insisting upon programmes for social service while especially taking into account the situation of those who are oppressed and marginalized.

Indeed, it is simply enthralling to look back and recall those days prior to Independence and take note of the hurdles even in the conceptualization process with regard to the subtle differences among the concepts of patriotism, nationalism, anti-imperialism and internationalism. It is not possible to go into the details here but let me refer to just one interesting example. Speaking of the time when the struggle for independence was in process, Tagore—the composer of our national song—said in one of his addresses to the students in Shantiniketan that during those days,

> our imaginations were filled with high-sounding words like Mother India. But we never really knew where to look for her. Patriotism was not more than a borrowed emotion, it was an addiction to an important idea. We acknowledged Mother India in her ancient glory. We failed to take account of her present miseries.[4]

Similarly, while construing many of the new glorious images of India (as a super power, etc.) today, we fail to recognize that the majority of Indians are not a part of that success story.

In brief, it is tempting to observe that there is no crisis of self-image in India, no dearth of conceptual resource in dealing with the various challenges of the present situation. The task, however, is to take cognizance of the depth of this resource and apply it more forcefully in support of the formation of a better-functioning, pluralistic society and especially in order to bring about changes in those specific areas of our national life where India is not quite 'shining'. A serious effort in this direction will also make transparent what India must really seek to achieve when relating herself to the assembly of nations.

Thus, it seems that the meta-philosophical guiding principle which lies at the core of the Indian culture is perhaps worth emulating today also for the sake of a deeper understanding of the self and the other—a topic much discussed among academicians. Generally speaking, the concern for recognizing the 'otherness' of the other in the theoretical discourse appears more to be for the sake of distinguishing the self from the other, since that is conceptually helpful for expressing a distinct self-image. However, in the projection of the core self-image of India that has been discussed above the presence of the other is significant not merely as a point of contrast, it is also for the sake of perceiving oneself as one among many and for insisting that the other must do the same in every context of empirical manifestations. It is noteworthy that this philosophical reading has been much explored in the context of the presence of plurality of religions in India but has not yet been adequately worked out within a trans-disciplinary discourse that deals with social, political and other cultural matters. It is essential to attempt that.

During the past two CCC conferences,[5] we did focus on the idea of human solidarity in connection with the notion of pluralism as a normative concept. It became increasingly transparent in the process of deliberation that pluralism is not tantamount to simply allowing diversity to surface but requires to be supported by a mechanism that promotes a sense for human solidarity. Otherwise, there is always the danger of falling into the trap of an extreme form of cultural relativism. The theoreticians who propound this latter view claim that no true communication is possible among the various groups since these are incommensurable. In some cases, the main concern seems to be how to contain this diversity in order to ensure the eventual dominance of the one with which these theoreticians identify. In both cases, the ideology of pluralism becomes a farce. These are all counter-images to what the core image of India stands for. We need to highlight the values that are embedded in this self-understanding, both for the sake of theory and practice.

At a time when there is finally a general acknowledgement of the increasing importance of India in the international context, it is disconcerting to find in some of the published material unusual concerns about how to catch up with the 'dragon' or how to simulate 'uncle Sam' rather than how to preserve this civilizational paradigm that the Indians under the leadership of some of the greatest minds struggled hard to protect from all intrusions of counter-images, even while the geographical boundaries of India changed dramatically. No doubt it would be valuable to discover and fortify similar images if these can be found elsewhere and ponder over how we all might learn to consolidate our energy into translating and implementing such ideas into the practical sphere of our collective lives.

The global scenario today is one where we are all seeking to create a partnership that has multiple dimensions. Attempts to forge new relationships in the domain of knowledge sharing, economy and politics and on other fronts are going on at an unusual speed. While engaged in this venture, it is worth repeating once again that construals of a self-image just as much as the process of articulations of one's self-understanding—no matter in which context—do reflect the way one perceives and interprets the otherness of the other, overtly or covertly. These are intimately interlinked. Interesting to recall here is the observation made by Wilhelm Halbfass, a German Indologist-cum-philosopher, that India has played a crucial role in the process of conceptualization of Europe's self-understanding particularly over the past several centuries. He emphasized that the manner in which Europe has 'questioned and defined itself' was significantly influenced by the way India has been viewed and imagined to be as a point of contrast and comparison.

However, it is quite amazing to see how with change of sociopolitical attitudes this interplay between the self and the other takes on diverse forms in different phases of history. Indeed, Tagore himself wrote about the crisis of identity in those days of social turmoil in Bengal, mentioning the sense of ambivalence that led to the swinging from finding everything indigenous to be distasteful to the passionate celebration of one's own heritage. Later he expressed his own view on this matter in unambiguous terms in a letter to C.F. Andrews: "I believe in the true meeting of the East and the West" and of "India's obligation to offer to others the hospitality of her best culture and India's right to accept from others their best".

Today, the encounter situation among various nations is quite different from what it has been even during the past century. It is evident that the days of overt claims of superiority of any single nation as standing a head above all others or that of 'ruling the waves' are over. Nevertheless, it is perhaps too soon to hope for cooperative leadership of the kind where no nation would like to see itself as being engaged in creating either within its own national or in the international sphere a situation that leads to despicable polarities of winners and losers, exploiters and exploited. More consolidated effort is needed for treating unanimously such a state of affairs as a counter-image to be shunned.

However, even if it might sound rather unrealistic today, human history does show in fact that change can happen in the social scene when what has been in the past the status quo becomes simply unthinkable. Recall that already in 1943, that is, shortly after the atrocious Bengal famine of 1942, Sri Aurobindo had observed that there was a time when it was taken for granted that the world would be divided among the rulers and the ruled but that the scene has begun to shift. He writes that "the right of all to liberty, both individuals and nations, the immorality of conquest and empire ... are new values, an evolutionary movement; this is a new Dharma which has only begun slowly and initially to influence practice...." He then expresses a warning and a hope that

> subject nations naturally accept the new Dharma and severely criticise the old imperialisms; it is to be hoped that they will practice what they now preach when they themselves become strong and rich and powerful. But the best will be if a new world-order evolves, even at first stumbingly or incompletely, which will make the old things impossible—a difficult task, but not absolutely impossible.

In short, it seems that the interaction between the ground realities and the aspirations in the different phases of history in different cultural soils mutually keep shaping the images of the self and the other. Let me conclude this essay with the hope that India would stick to her core self-image. I am inclined to think that whoever governs India now or will do so in the future would strive to keep it alive as it inspires attitudes and actions for bridging the gap between the self and the other. As we keep groping to find authentic backing for pluralism and struggle to implement such insights through institutional mechanisms, our success will determine India's place in the world assembly of nations. Perhaps some thoughts in this vein inspired Nicholas Roerich to make the startling remark: "If India were India, She could lead the World."

NOTES AND REFERENCES

1. One can find elaborate explanations and arguments in support of this idea in the texts of Advaita Vedanta.
2. Although there are other intricacies that would require elaboration in this context, such as the issues of the role of the secular state in a multi-religious society entailing when the norm of non-interference must give way to timely intervention or how to compare this understanding of religious freedom with that found in the treaty of Westphalia, etc.
3. As is known, one of the principal characters of this work actually represents Tagore's own political stand who—despite his patriotism—stands for a refusal to compromise with loyalty to nationalism as the highest value. This deals with a tragic story of the struggle and defeat of cosmopolitanism by the forces of nationalism and ethnocentrism.
4. 'Rabindranath Tagore and His Contemporary Relevance', in Uma Dasgupta (ed.) (India: Parabas).
5. I organized these CCC international conferences in New Delhi in 2006 and 2009.

2

Two Indias: Gandhiji and Modern India

Johan Galtung

Gandhi was killed not far from where we are right now by a Pune Brahmin, Godse, and I was that 17-year-old boy in Norway who cried when hearing the news. Something unheard of had happened. But I did not know why I cried, and wanted to know more. Who was Gandhi? I became a Gandhi scholar, inspired, as assistant and co-author, by the late Arne Naess' seminal work, extracting from Gandhi's works and words the political ethics of his action as a norm system.[1]

To me, the image of India I love is the image of Gandhi. I know perfectly well that there are other Indias. And Ashis Nandy sensitized me to why the court proceedings against Godse were kept secret: because his arguments were, briefly put, that Gandhi stood in the way of a modern India, with industrialization, booming cities, growth, trade, a strong army—the whole package. Very different from Gandhi's sarvodaya villages, self-sufficient, linked by 'oceanic circles', focused on spiritual rather than material growth. And very similar to the Buddhist image of the sangha, confirming Gandhi's idea that he may actually have been a Buddhist—without any vertical ranking of castes. These last points, the link to Buddhism and the rejection of caste, may have been on top of Godse's motivation.

That modern India was also Nehru's India, with a socialist, London School of Economics (LSE) touch of Harold Laski to it. Nehru and Gandhi may have found some meeting points in theory and words, if not in reality, and certainly not in a Soviet reality very remote from Gandhi's world. Gandhi was instrumentalized by Congress to get rid of the Britons preaching against caste, and India became independent, with a disastrous partition mainly caused by Lord Mountbatten, free to enter modernity, and to keep caste. The Congress Party got the cake, and could eat it too.

So I see two Indias, Gandhiji and modernity, knowing well there are more. Which one is self-image and which one is counter-image is not for me to know or judge. Two Indian civilizations, with much clash and little dialogue, and dwarfs eliminating India's greatest son. Some time ago we could find books on, and even by, Gandhi at the new airport; today we find books on business administration. A non-dialogue of two civilizations within one country is here carried out by a non-Indian.

But on behalf of millions touched by the genius of the Gandhi modern India expelled, like traditional India did with another genius coming out of roughly the same land, the Buddha. The image of India abroad is still largely shaped by Gandhi, a Vaisya prime minister's son, a lawyer trained in England, struggling with the drives of sex and food, finding his *brahmacharya*. Most Indian themes—with as much or more claim on whatever we call India as the present Americanized growth machine for upper castes and some more, at the expense of growing inequality and the suffering of the one-third of the world's starving who live in one country, India—were linked to a falling global empire, the USA, and a regional declining empire, Israel.

Linked by violence, all three: direct violence by acts of commission; structural violence churning out far more suffering than direct violence, upheld by acts of omission; and cultural violence legitimizing either or both. Indo-European class structure gives the Brahmins the cultural violence, the Kshatriyas the direct violence and the Vaisyas the structural violence—unleashing them on common people, women and chosen aliens. A tradition of direct violence plus being high or low in a structural violence pyramid plus deriving legitimacy from a divine mandate or whatever predicts well the four most belligerent countries over the last one thousand years: the USA, Israel, the Ottoman Empire and the UK. Watch your friends, India. And watch the dangers of guilt by cooperation and association.

Gandhiji will survive this perverted Indian modernity. He stood for Gandhi's Four: satyagraha, Swaraj, swadeshi and sarvodaya. They carry a complete approach to sustainable peace and development.

Satyagraha: Holding on to the Satya is equal to Truth–Love–God trinity, his unity-of-human beings. As fact, truth; as togetherness, compassion, love; and as embodying the divine. Ahimsa, non-violence, reflects this badly; so Gandhi, a little more than 100 years ago, coined that new term. He drew on *vasudaiva kuttumbakam*, the world is my family, very Indian, but not practiced by the believers in 700,000 soldiers in Kashmir, in driving tribals and casteless off the land, in killing Naxalites with drones and in bad relations with all neighbours.

Swaraj: The self of identity and power-over-self join in self-rule. Gandhi praised openness, yet not being blown off one's feet. Be rooted, but deepen the rootedness. Develop yourself, but be a spirit in command of ego, a concept beyond any independence ceremony with flags lowered and raised. Gandhi did not attend, he fought Lord Mountbatten—twisted partition with its devastating consequences.

Swadeshi: Self-made, to be in command of meeting own needs for food, shelter, clothing. No to English textiles and Yes to khadi. Gandhi, against Nehru, collected money not to harm Bombay merchants.

Sarvodaya: The uplift of the poor, inspired by Gandhi's dictum—there is enough for everybody's need, but not for everybody's greed.

Gandhiji for need, modernity for greed; Gandhi for local self-reliance, modernity for unlimited trade; Gandhi for building own identity, modernity for Americanization as neo-nirvana; Gandhi for non-violent conflict resolution, modernity for police, military, war.

India's modernity may head for a crash landing, so quite a blessing to have Gandhiji on the reserve shelf. There is space for both. But right now both Delhi and the Naxalites would be better off with Gandhi's Four than with state and non-state terror.

These four small words shed much light on Gandhi's concept of power. It is not Western power-over-others, by military power (sticks), economic power (carrots), cultural power (imposed identity) or political power (because it is do decided), pitting one set of power against the other for balance or for conquest. Actually, the West never believed in balance as mechanical equality but as being in the black, having an excess, for safety or dominance. Equality and equity were never the formula for West–Rest relations.

Gandhi's power was power-over-self, making yourself immune to somebody else's power. Sarvodaya lifts us into dignity; swadeshi makes us self-reliant, independent; Swaraj makes us our own decision-makers.

Our selves are exactly that, Our selves, our identities. And satyagraha gives us a tool far superior to 'fighting it out'.

Let us now look at five approaches to conflict at the meso- and macro-levels, between major social groups, nations and states: interstate warfare, guerrilla, negotiation, non-violence and satyagraha.

(1) Interstate warfare, institutionalized violence in uniform.
    The West dates the state system to the Peace of Westphalia of 1648 which was no peace at all but legitimized interstate wars for victory to dictate the terms of peace. This approach to conflict is today on the decline, probably not because of its irrationality but because of the decrease in salience of the state system, yielding to regions and corporate globalization above, and to local authorities and nations below, the level of states. Nations are built around idiom and religion, history-time and geography-space and serve as powerful identity-builders, mobilizing more readiness to die than for states in a tepid state system mainly in equilibrium, with some territorial clashes here and there. With an average of 10 nations per state, and most states ruled by one dominant nation, the shift of point of gravity for conflict and violence to nations is palpable.

(2) Guerrilla warfare, continuation of warfare by violent means.
    19 April 1775: Shooting from behind the fences, barns, walls, from inside the houses, reloading, hurrying—new type of warfare—fighting like savages. Well, the savages won the US War of Independence after these clashes on the Boston–Concord road, and the result was the USA today fighting other 'savages' with their former UK masters, repeating history. Former savages graduated to state terrorists, new emerging savages are referred to as terrorists, like Goebbels did—their violence being negligible relative to state terrorism.

(3) Negotiation, continuation of warfare by verbal means.
    The word debate, with is connotation of beating with words, a major technique being to catch the other side in a contradiction, between facts and facts, facts and values, values and values or whatever. Arguments are based on deductions from first principles and data to prove the superiority of one's own

position. The idea is that the party with the best arguments wins. If the parties are relatively equal, there is room for a compromise usually satisfying nobody; and if they are unequal, some principle of proportionality relative to their power will enter—up to and including the total superiority of a victor, dictating victor's peace. Debates will move the gravity of power from the Kshatriya of (1), and the Sudra of (2), to the Brahmin, like a Habermas using a good university seminar as a model.

(4)   Non-violence, continuation of warfare by non-violent means. Non-violence adds to meetings with resolutions, demonstrations with risks. Without risks, no non-violence; the willingness to incur risks for one's cause is supposed to convert the opponent, creating a loser. The violent opponent is deprived of a role partner who refuses to react to violence with violence and to act inside a violent structure. No doubt, this often works like for human rights serving only one conflict party, with little attention to the loser.

(5)   Satyagraha, a holistic approach to conflict resolution. The four approaches above are based on parties and how to regulate their relations whereas satyagraha sees an antagonism as an artificial division in the unity-of-humans, the goal being to restore that unity. Hence, the antagonist in conflict is treated like oneself according to the 69 proposed Gandhi norms. Being parts of the same spiritual unity, this makes sense, but does not exclude completely the other approaches. Thus, Gandhi preferred the courage of the violent Kshatriya to the non-violence of the coward, promoting the idea of the non-violent heroic warrior, thereby combining two Indian themes.

Building on Gandhi, standing on his shoulders, the TRANSCEND method also sees a conflict from above by engaging in searching dialogues with the parties, one at the time so that they can express themselves freely; mapping the conflict—which are the parties, their goals and their means—testing goals and means for their legitimacy according to law, human rights and basic needs and then trying to bridge legitimate goals in a vision of a new reality. This is not 'win-win' but 'both-and-and', transcending beyond their visions.

Much empathy is needed with all parties, much verbal non-violence being constructive, creative and concrete rather than moralistic and critical, and above all, much creativity in conceiving of compelling visions. The power of the vision, the dream, building on what was good in the past and the horrors of violent struggle compared to the nightmare of what might happen with no mediation quite often works.

The method is presented in the author's *Transcend and Transform: An Introduction to Conflict Work*;[2] also see *50 Years: 100 Peace & Conflict Perspectives*[3] and editorials for Transcend Media Service.[4] The next sections deal with two of them, the Kashmir imbroglio and the poor versus rich conflict—as examples, and as products of, non-Gandhian Indian modernity.

There are literally hundreds of dialogues behind each of them.

And that brings to an end this overview of the contradiction between two images of India. Modernity has excluded Gandhism at an enormous loss to India. But the conclusion is by no means that modernity is bad and Gandhism perfect. As indicated above, there is ample room for both compromise and transcendence.

Thus, starting with sarvodaya—very efficient for the uplift of the poor, but devoid of pluralism and dynamism. As they say about township in the US Midwest: "If you have seen one of them you have seen them all." Indian modernity may be accused of an excess rather than deficit of pluralism and dynamism—for the few, the rich basically, but not only.

And swadeshi can be combined with trade, but then mostly with countries at the same technical level to avoid dependencies, raising each other together, like countries in east South East Asia did.

And Swaraj does not stop at the individual and local levels but can also includes the national, regional and global, but then with full respect for the Swaraj, in the West called freedom, autonomy, of the 'lower' levels, something modernity is not good at.

Finally, satyagraha. Gandhi did not argue against police, but would probably have preferred police of the dialogical type, trying to identify root causes of violence rather than ritualistically re-establishing law and 'order' predestined to reproduce the violence. And, to sit non-violently in front of the violence of non-empathic, violent fascists are irresponsible. Better flight than fight.

And so on, and so forth. So much could emerge from an internal and equitable Indian dialogue of civilizations. But that was not to be. Modernity eliminated Gandhism, and the latter often became dogmatic and inflexible. Gandhi was put on a pedestal as Father of the Nation, of Swaraj only. May he re-emerge in the Indian consciousness and reality as the very vital force he always was.

KASHMIR FOLLOW-UP: A TRANSCEND PERSPECTIVE (MAY 2006 REPORT)

There are strong forces in the world today—such as an Anglo-American-led economic globalization, military globalization by state terrorist and terrorist means and regionalization—partly in response to these globalizations.

One such regionalization is South Asian Association for Regional Cooperation (SAARC), not very dynamic but filled with potentials like a South Asian Free Trade Area (SAFTA). Another is an Islamic region, potentially from Casablanca to Mindanao, including an Islamic economic globalization to counteract the other three. Running West–East, and SAARC North–South in Asia, the conflict potential is considerable. So is the solution potential, like SAARC and an Islamic community joining forces within a South–South and a global context. We are talking about 1.3–1.5 billion humans—twice. With another 1.3 billion, Chinese are very close.

In the centre of this is the problematic India–Pakistan nucleus of the subcontinent. The relation is not 'neither peace nor war' but 'some peace, some war'. The relation cries for a normalization which, if brought about in an equitable manner, could be immensely popular with the populations in both countries. The issues, such as Kashmir, divided Punjab, divided Bengal, etc., mainly derive from the 1947 Partition of the subcontinent more than 60 years ago.

Normalization, given the strong forces impinging upon India–Pakistan, becomes mandatory. And there is no military solution between two nuclear powers, only a stalemate. The fact that it is not really mutually hurtful should not be taken as an excuse for inaction. The world is catching up with India–Pakistan. One problem is Kashmir as an issue that may ignite powder kegs beyond India–Pakistan. A more positive view of Kashmir would focus on all the creative forces that could be released if the parts of Kashmir could come closer together.

Sixty years of unstable equilibrium have taught us that the Kashmir problem does not go away by itself. And yet it is hard to believe that a reasonable settlement could not be arrived at that could actually give the parties—Kashmiris, Pakistanis and Indians—even more than some of them are demanding separately, with a little flexibility, and some out-of-the-box thinking. The land and possibly sea connections opening up are already significant steps in that direction, but more has to follow for those promising openings not to become sources of frustration rather than gratification.

How about a Kashmir Area Free Trade Association (KAFTA), an increasingly borderless area modelled after European Free Trade Association (EFTA) in Europe, with free flow of persons, goods services and ideas across borders dwindling in significance. With a Steering Committee of, say, 10 persons, three Kashmiris, three Pakistanis, three Indians and one from SAARC. In due course of time, KAFTA could become a part of SAFTA, as a precursor or as a consequence. But given the urgency of the Kashmir problem, sooner rather than later.

The KAFTA could be a part of a settlement that could cover all seven zones, and give all residents the right of free passage, like, for instance, in the Nordic community. A common identity card for the area in addition to passports might take the process one step further. The rights of investment and settlement might be included or follow later. An assembly giving legitimacy to the Steering Committee should not be excluded—in due course of time.

With SAARC as an, admittedly weak, umbrella for KAFTA, and KAFTA as an umbrella for a possible Kashmiri community, some disaggregation could take place more easily, given this type of assurance that what belongs geographically and historically together could nevertheless also grow together. Thus, Jammu and Ladakh are today parts of India, and Azad Kashmir is de facto a part of Pakistan.

These facts, possibly with some minor revisions, should be recognized by all parties concerned. To give the Line of Control (LoC) de jure status may then follow after a trial period of X years for any settlement. The only positive outcome derived from 60 years of quarrel might actually be that in the course of events, both countries somehow have gotten used to accepting what to all three parties was unacceptable, making the LoC a part of the solution, not of the problem.

What remains is The Valley. Several formulas are available. They might all include Srinagar as the seat of an increasingly beneficial KAFTA that would have to prove itself as a lynchpin in a settlement. The current Indian sovereignty (in Pakistan referred to as 'occupation', the term used in India for the Pakistani control of Azad Kashmir) could gradually yield to a joint security authority with Pakistani and Indian—and increasingly Kashmiri—forces (by and large with the same English military culture) doing the job together. Whether as part of India or as condominium, The Valley would have a high level of autonomy, gradually developing its own institutions. How about making Siachen a peace park, off limits to army—a place to be celebrated as a symbol of peace rather than deplored as an outcome of war—with all parties cooperating in making it attractive as one more part of the tremendous tourism opportunities offered by this highly attractive part of the common human heritage? This is not a question of taking some problematic first steps; they have already been taken. It is a question of follow-up, at a pace better adjusted to the magnitude not only of the problems but also of the promises that would follow in the wake of normalization. Energy supply would meet energy demand as it should between neighbours, so would water, so would a host of commodities and products—and human ties, as amply testified by what happens when the two Punjabs come closer together. Keep going. The sky is the limit.

KASHMIR: A PEACE AND CONFLICT PERSPECTIVE (JANUARY 1998 REPORT)

(1) **Process.** The Simla Accord in 1972 mandated Indo-Pak bilateral negotiations which so far have not delivered peace. If the approach is not wrong but incomplete, then add the following:

(a) South Asian Association for Regional Cooperation setting
(b) Indo-Pak Non-governmental Organization (NGO) roundtables for dialogue negotiation

(c)   Outside mediators, governmental
(d)   Outside mediators, non-governmental, individuals
(e)   United Nations

All could be tried, and simultaneously for synergy effects.

If (c) is attempted big powers with obvious interests in the area, such as the USA and China (seen as pro-Pakistan) and the UK and Russia (seen as pro-India, and then the UK is also the former colonial power) should have the good sense of staying away. So should United Nations Security Council (UNSC) as the sum of member biases is not likely to be creative and useful.

(2)   **Outcome.** The following is an image of possible outcomes that may one day in some form be acceptable to parties in the conflict:

(a)   Differential centre–periphery relations in the Indian Union

For the centre in New Delhi to have the same relations to all states makes sense in a colonial-bureaucratic setting, but may produce continued violence. That violence should not be construed as a demand for secession-independence when what is being asked for is autonomy in some fields. Thus, in Western Europe the countries not European Union (EU) members all cooperate with EU, and two EU members (Denmark and the UK) have autonomy in very important fields. India is twice the size and more complex. Kashmir is not the only part interested in negotiating, say, less federal, more confederal ties: so might Nagaland and some others. The process will be painful. But 'in strength there is weakness, and in weakness strength'; flexibility will serve them all.

(b)   Differential yet cohesive policies to the parts of Kashmir

An undifferentiated policy for a Kashmir with three or four parts makes sense only in a colonial-bureaucratic setting, but guarantees continued violence. That violence should not be construed as a demand for secession-independence when autonomy in some fields may be the solution, ruling out three options: full integration with Pakistan (Jamat, Hizbul

Mujahideen), full integration with India (the Instrument of Accession) and fully independent state of Kashmir (the Hurriyat Conference).

A differentiated policy could include the following: if Jammu and Ladakh want integration with India, so be it; if Azad Kashmir wants integration with Pakistan, so be it; for The Valley, if autonomy and devolution within India on the lines of the 1952 or 1974 constitutional provisions is what is wanted, so be it.

For cohesiveness, the following might be useful:

(i)   Indo-Pak transitional condominium for The Valley
(ii) Indo-Pak cooperation in softening the LoC
(iii) Civil society cooperation across the border—LoC: Union of families, cultural cooperation, local economic cooperation—this is needed everywhere, also to overcome the effects of globalization
(iv) A Greater Kashmir community of all parts, with open borders, the KAFTA, linked to New Delhi–Islamabad

(c)   Collateral issues

This does not address arms merchants and mercenaries wanting profits and youth in alienating societies seeing violence and rape not only as 'the best show, but the only show in town'. But they will dwindle away. And the Siachen Glacier could become a human heritage monument dedicated to peace.

In short, differentiate and weave together as a community.

THE MILLENNIUM DEVELOPMENT GOALS: A PEACE AND CONFLICT PERSPECTIVE (THE MILLENNIUM DEVELOPMENT GOALS BY 2015 ARE WELL CHOSEN, EVEN LAUDABLE)

(a) Eradicate extreme poverty and hunger, reducing by one half those who live on less than $1 a day and those who are starving; (b) ensure that all boys and girls complete elementary school; (c) promote gender equality and empower women, removing the proportion difference of girls and boys in elementary school; (*d*) reduce child mortality, reduce by two-thirds the proportion of children who die before they are five years old; (*e*) improve maternal health, reducing by three-fourths the proportion of women who die in connection with pregnancy; (*f*) combat HIV/AIDS, malaria, reversing the deadly diseases; (*g*) ensure environmental sustainability, reducing by one half the people who live without access to safe water and improving the living conditions for at least 100 million living in slums; (*h*) develop a global partnership for development, increasing development assistance, just trade and debt forgiveness.

They address basic human needs, privilege the most needy, emphasize gender parity, focus on environment and global equity. There is no 'trickling down' when 'time is ripe'. Right on target. The problem is that they are unachievable given the disconnect between Millennium Development Goals (MDGs) and an absurd economic system producing 125,000 deaths a day from starvation and preventable/curable diseases. One has to yield, so far the basic needs.

And yet it can be done.

NOTES AND REFERENCES

1. For my own version of that system, please see my book, 1995. *The Way is the Goal* (Ahmedabad: Navajivan) (reprinted on the back of the cover pages of 2010. *A Theory of Conflict* [Transcend University Press]).
2. London, Boulder CO: Pluto, Paradigm, 2003; in 25 languages so far. For more advanced approaches, see the books published by Transcend University Press, www.transcend.org/tup, especially TUP 7–10. The smaller TUP handbooks are more accessible.
3. This is TUP #1 from 2008, in a sense the 'flagship' of TRANSCEND, a non-governmental NGO for peace, development and environment mediation.
4. Weekly since March 2008, see www.transcend.org/tms

3

Time, Space and Self-image in Indic Culture

Lokesh Chandra

Biology, ecology, history and cosmosophy have been the *terra cognita* that has reverberated as the self-image. Our quest begins with the animal origins of human identity. The inward compulsion in animate beings to possess and defend space has been the mysterious flow of energy and resolve that culminated as the self-image.

Five propensities dominate Indic thought: (*a*) love of the land—the territorial imperative; (*b*) sacredness of all life—no heathens; (*c*) divinity of nature—no red in tooth and claw; (*d*) the divine within us—no external God; (*e*) unity *in* diversity—no chosen people and fundamentalism. Self-image is the inward focus that becomes our plenum, strengthened by a counter-image, in ever-renewing epistemological backdrops.

Self-image is the inward focus that becomes the plenum of a people, while a counter-image is the strengthening of this vision that sharpens the enlightened 'playfulness' to outcompete others in ideas. It is the inexpressible sense of 'we' when the heart remembers home. Self-image is one's own idea or picture of oneself, especially in relation to others. It is *asmitii* or the fact that I exist, act and live my full-throttle life. It is the antidote to 'surviving' that seeks to find arguments sans end, month after month, year after year, to do nothing, to choose delay as pleasant inaction. The Russian word for work *rabotaet* is cognate to the Sanskrit root *rabh*, which means 'to kill'. Rationalization of the negative is to postpone action. A self-image is a creative, action-intensive, sociopolitically committed identity that harmonizes the past, present and future in an ordered system of development. Self-image is a strong sense of internal balance that becomes an inspiration to act, to dream and to attain perfection in all discoveries and achievements. All people have a history that endows them with characteristic genes, which give them a strong feeling to endure, to succeed and to benefit the collective in a flow that owns the new ways of others, without losing the spirit and poise of one's culture.

Self-image demands a sharp cleavage of (*a*) amity versus enmity, (*b*) discord versus concord, (*c*) self versus the other, (*d*) variance versus convergence, (*e*) universal versus distinctive uniqueness, (*f*) geographic specificity versus fuzzy globalism, (*g*) one's own history versus infinity of time. The lack of 'one's own text' subverts inward focus and fosters anarchy of precise ideas so that failures and traumas are rationalized as inclusivity. The powerful incentive to decidability suffers. To quote David Hilbert,[1] "We hear within us the perpetual call: There is the problem. Seek its solution."

Self-image and counter-image are alien to Indic thought. India has always thought of the infinite and the universal, so that the valorization of time and the finite bounds of concentrated creativity and dynamic activity became diaphanous elements of life. The Atharva Veda says: *samudro asmi vidhannana*, 'the Unbounded Ocean am I', wherein personal uniqueness and collective self-perspective become the unity of noble ideals without a secular counterpart to ameliorate our lives. The catharsis of karma is complete and non-attachment is the terrible sublime. It is the 'sacred disorder', leading to the conceptualization of life as *duhkha*. The immoderate, gigantic sublime does not make the world a home, a home of constant striving. We have to seek the mathematical lines of force so that the world is always brought back to the measure of Man, where the linearity of thought has to be chastened by the sinuous logic of life, in which the finite, the measurable, the bounded becomes the quest of all-embracing existence, ever-rising higher in a sustained effort to develop by hard work. The last century has seen India lose its self-image and succumb to a multilaterality of freewheeling attitude towards culture, language and political perceptions that subvert our very identity. Processes dominate over substance and we accept all but our own text.

Some definitive dimensions of self-image in India have been:

(1) Love of one's land (*punya-bhumi*). In the Rig Veda, earth is the
      boundless, mother, great, firm and shining. She is celebrated
      along with the sky—*dyava-prithivi*.

          Earth is the mother of man, and heaven the father (*dyaus
      pita prithivi mata*). The territorial imperative is fundamental to
      life. The biological sciences accept the concept of territory as a
      genetically determined form of behaviour. "A territory is an area
      of space, whether of water or earth or air, which an animal or
      group of animals defends as an exclusive preserve...." It is a force
      that shapes our lives in countless ways. Sanctity of the earth, love
      of the land induces spiritual universality. It is the end result of
      a long agricultural tradition. The Semitic religions crystallized
      in arid zones and are the end products of pastoralism, which
      is violent and predatory. Pastoralism is defence-intensive. For
      cohesion, it seeks a high Military and Political Participation Ratio
      (MPPR). Indians could preserve their native spiritual roots as
      they were wedded to their land. An agriculturist would grab the
      land of another only if the land were scarce and if he disposed the
      labour to till it. Agriculturism is labour-intensive. It is a world
      of sharing, of humane distillation, of intrinsic multiformity and
      of the freedom of choice. It values the rights of humans to be
      'sculptors of themselves', as well as a vast variance of peoples as
      against a chosen people.

(2) Sacredness of all life. Intense concern for the sanctity of all life
      and the interdependence of all sentient and stationary life as
      well as inanimate nature is the hallmark of Indian thought. The
      worship of woods and waters, of trees, stocks and stones, of fire
      and animals go back to ancient Vedic rites. The life cycle of the
      humans was dependent on the festival cycle of the agricultural
      seasons. The deities of the embodied state of human life found
      harmony in theurgy, that is, communication with the divine by
      external rites. They celebrated man's place in and dependence
      on nature, a metaphor of the Divine. The summer and winter
      solstices mirror the yearly cycle of spring and autumn. They are
      the *purusa*, 'the Supreme Being', and *prakriti*, 'Nature'.

The human and the Divine participate in ecstatic song and dance. In the Rig Veda, the inanimate and animate are divine. The Divine steed symbolic of the sun and fire, the cow as beams of the dawn, the kine as the waters, are symbols of many-splendoured life. The phenomena of nature, aerial and celestial, and the earth itself are deities in the Rig Veda. Rivers, mountains, plants, sacrificial implements are as mighty as heaven. They are invoked to drive away demons and destruction and to bestow wealth and offspring. The forest is a deity under the name of *Aranyani* in the Rig Veda 10.146: striking a postmodern note on the conservation of ecological balance. The immensity of creation wherein the kingdoms of plants and animals, stones and natural phenomena harmonize with the Human is the divinity of the biosphere. Vishnu incarnates as fish, boar, tortoise. Buddha is born in several animal genera in the one *atakas* to gain perfection in the six transcendent *paramitas*.

Indian thought is a seeking of the symbols of consciousness, a way to wisdom, a resonating integrity of the multiple. It is an interface with the timeless and cosmic. No commandments but awakened awareness, no dogmas but dialogue, no ideology but ideas, so that tiny pebbles gathered on the shoreline of life become fine like pearls. When we carry these pebbles back home to our hearts, intertwined with them will be the sea of consciousness in our sleeves. It is the flow of spiritual culture and material civilization in the rhythms of the universe, evolving into the wholeness of an inner unity. Our quest is eternal, even beyond our within. We wander through all the outer worlds to reach the innermost shrine at the end. We are pilgrims to the yonder shore, we live to have something to outlive. In a world where science has become cannibalistic and humanity has become edible, will technology devour the significance of human existence? As the Isha Upanishad says: "You should therefore only take what is really necessary for yourself, which is set aside for you. You should not take anything else, because you know to whom it belongs." The world will have to be "the land of duty, not the land of enjoyment" (Mahatma Gandhi). A Sanskrit text says: "The whole life of these trees is to serve. With their leaves, flowers, fruits, branches, roots, shade, fragrance, sap, bark, wood and finally even their ashes and coal, they exist for the purpose of others." Trees and animals, forests and rivers are divine symbols of life, and we humans are part of that interdependent whole. Forest is as deep a culture as spiritualism. We may define three categories of forests: the forest that provides prosperity (*shri-vana*), the forest where sages contemplate and seek truth (*tapo-vana*) and the great natural forest (*maha-vana*) where all life finds shelter.

(3)   The divinity of nature. In Samkhya philosophy, *prakriti* or Nature and *purusa* or The Transcendent Being are, respectively, the visible realm and the transcendental foundation. Mind is among the material phenomena illumined by transcendental consciousness (*chit*). It is Eternal Realities (*satya* from the root as 'to exist') that give our existence both meaning and value. *Rita* of the Rig Veda is the cosmic order that is natural as well as ethical. It is impersonal: it has no personification. It exists independently of the gods, who maintain the cosmic paradigm to protect the world against chaos and ignorance. *Rita* is the cosmic rhythm and *satya* is the flow of life. Man is free to order his life in concordance with moral or divine laws and practical needs: he has the freedom of choice as well as the responsibility for his actions. This is the theory of karma. He is not born in sin, he inherits no sins and only his own actions absolve him or involve him in sin or in merit.

The five elements (*panca-bhuta*) are: earth, water, fire, air and ether. They are the ground and activators of purification and intensification of life. Today as pollution of the ecology proceeds at a rapid pace, Indian rites of divinizing heaven and earth gain a new meaning. The cult of the sun, the celebration of the summer solstice, the Moon God who traverses the sky (namely, the morning and evening stars who form the Vedic Asvins) are our links with Nature, which have to be respected and protected. Offerings to 'Mother Earth' ensure that forests will function as lungs of cities, gardens as welfare cycles and fields of crops as life cycles. Humans adore natural surrounds so that the social context functions on a cosmic level. The opening words of the Rig Veda pay homage to the fire: *agnim ide purohitam*. They are the first words of the Indo-European people that have lived on for millennia. Yajna fires kindled on river banks were the flow of the mind. The flowing rivers gave the idea of constant progress: "where the clear stream of reason has not lost its way into the dreary desert sand" (Tagore). The sands are the birthplace of monocentrism. The infinite universe is a cathode and the perceiving consciousness of humans is the receiving anode.

(4) Love of history. The Eternal is value and the New is meaning. To India, millennia of Time are 'living space', the subtle and profound unseen of Becoming. The sanctity of Eternity is reflected in myths and sacred rites, in lyrical survivals and poignant attachment to the Perennial (*sanatana*). History is the deeper ground of our existence. Poet Goethe says:

> He whose vision cannot cover
> History's three thousand years
> Must in other darkness hover.

Time resonates with the genes in our body, handed down from our ancestors of the remote past, as centuries cast their spiritual rays on us. The *sanatana* is the eternal sacred.

(5) Unity in diversity. Unity and diversity are the two banks of the river of culture and civilization, of the heart and the mind, wherein flows the multiple in freedom. The flow is constant change as well as perennial diversity and richness of unfolding reality. The word Hindu means the great river Sindhu, its ever-flowing waters. It remind us of the play *The Bacchae* by Euripides: "Many are the shapes of things divine." It is a touch with the depths, a new turn, a re-turn to polytheism. David L. Miller says:

> It would seem inevitable that the God of the monotheistic theology would die, that He would suffer an ineluctable demise. The imperialism of the mind ... cannot forever endure.... Thinking monotheistically about the deepest matters of the heart and spirit cannot put man in touch with life.

We inhabit a spiritual universe as a continuing relationship between 'inside' and 'outside'. There is no 'inside' without an 'outside'. It has to be a continuing realization in the dream-space of humans. Without diminution of religious autonomies, we will have to own the 'other'. Alterity or otherness will be integral to humanity. No universal mission as a management of the world, but the acceptance of pluralism as well as respect for multiplicity. We have to pass from de facto plurality to pluralism. It has to be an authentic human plentitude of various strands, held together by mutual respect. The thoughtless imposition of one universal validity can dehumanize. Humanity can function mainly on its intrinsic multiformity, by vindicating respect for each other. Without abolishing constitutive polarities, we can awaken the feeling of human solidarity in a pluralistic world. We can labour in the vineyards of sharing than wherein the grapes of wrath are stored.

After millennia of separate histories, the cultures of mankind now suddenly find themselves in a common situation. Natural resources dwindling, water table going down every year, pollution levels reaching critical levels, social relationships being dominated by egotism and national frontiers in meaningless array: all threaten human life itself. The technosphere is on a collision course against the biosphere.

Humanity needs a dynamic transformation. It has to be a meaningful arrangement of different orders. A common situation cannot be and should not be a single syndrome. It has to be a symbiosis of the multiple, a polycentric consciousness. Biodiversity is the supreme law of nature. There are over a hundred thousand species of flora and fauna in India alone, more than a lakh of forms of plant and animal life in our country. Likewise, the spiritual life has to divine the several meanings, the fuzzy wisdom of nature, the light of the Many and to image the sacrament that enshrines the Multiple, the Changing, the Silent. Theodiversity is an inescapable corollary to the astounding discoveries in science and their universal applications in technology.

(6)   Life is divine. Indian thought has many dimensions, accepts change as integral to spiritual evolution. It is beyond time and is not hampered by the divinity of revelation. It has no dogmas and owns dialogue with the many, as well as the awakening of consciousness from within. Man transcends by the indwelling divinity in him, rather than be guided by an anachronistic formulation that was relevant in the age and in the context in which it arose but became outdated by new developments. It is the Divine within that grows through visualization, contemplation, meditation. It is beyond matter and beyond mind, and irradiates human consciousness. It is the incandescence of Being. Monotheism is obedience to an externality, to a power that was conceived in ages past and cannot be redeemed by change in the context of the present, in the context of our lives. It is a condescension of God rather than illumination of our Being. In India, the Divine is within us and we ascend as part of human transcendence. In monotheism, God is beyond us and we have to condition ourselves to its tenets. Religion is from *religare*, 'to bind up'. It binds us to a belief that we have to accept, and at the same time we have to own that it is True. It is not illumination. It does not evolve from inner wholeness. It demands unquestioning acceptance. It is communication to a lesser being, from a higher being God through an intermediary. In polytheism, life is divine, nature is divine and the individual seeks his transfiguration into the majesty of the Divine. In Sanskrit it is said: *na adevo devam arcayet*, that is, we should divinize ourselves to worship the Divine. While in the Christian tradition, the flesh is sin, and the genesis of humanity is a Fall, in the Rig Veda we are inherently Divine. In India, all Life is divine: men, animals and trees share the sanctity of life. The trees do not move but they stand. Animals are *pashu* in Sanskrit, from the root *pash*, 'to see': they see and respond to stimuli by instinct. The English word *man* is from the root *man*, 'to think' (compare Hindi *man*, *manas*, 'mind', *manana*, 'thinking'). Humans have the higher faculty of thought, of retaining that thought as memory and learning, so that it becomes a basis for

new ideas. It is a continuing process of evolution of ideas, the rise of proto-technology and technology, of interacting with natural forces and cosmic phenomena. In the realm of the spirit, humans realize the unity of all manifestations of Life, of sharing existence on different levels, in harmony with the world around us. This vast existence is the goddess Gaia of the Greeks. Gaia is the earth, the cow, the flowing river, the shining rays of the sun. It is a multi-semantic word from the Rig Vedic *ga*, *gau*, *go* with these meanings. In the monotheistic systems, there is Only One Truth, namely, God. He is sacred and his Revelation has an exclusive sanctity. This monocentric view has brought us to our present plight of the pollution of the environment. It calls for a new paradigm: *para*, 'beyond' plus *digm*, 'to show': a seeing beyond, the epic of the multiple vision wherein life is not sin, but sanctity. Lord Buddha speaks of his pre-incarnations in the Jatakas when he was born as a king, a sage, a bird, an animal, an aquatic animal, etc. Buddhism posits that all living beings are capable of the highest Bodhi or Enlightenment, and as such are 'potential Buddhas', in Sanskrit *Buddhankura*, 'Sprouting Buddhas'.

(7)   Indian thought has many centres of being and becoming, and thus owns both the temporal and spatial dimensions. Time and space can condition existence and transcendence. What may be true in the desert may not be so in the lush green lands. Monotheism arose in the arid zone of the earth where the featureless desert inscribed its monotone, its One recognition and gave a determinate focus. The uninhabitable landscape dictated: life and nature were divorced from the Divine. The desert imbued with its tyranny of burning sands could not be a holy place. It was a registration of anomaly. It gave an Absolute of an unchanging beyond, of The One, as it was itself One unchanging. Hardly a person is seen in the arid expanses. It invoked dehumanization in the euphemism of a Divine Revelation. Polytheism is a product of agricultural landscapes wherein a place is imbued with significance, where man finds food for his body from the green fertility of the land, water from a well, lake or river to quench his thirst, the wood, forest or tree

to share its 'growing' with him, and the height of a hill or peak to uplift his being. These fluidities of nature, as distinguished from the fixities of the desert, provide man extensive foci of veneration and worship.

Polytheism was the origin of polycentrism where the many were owned and honoured. It was a system of sharing among men, among tribes, between humans and nature and of a relationship of the human, cosmic and divine: a cosmotheandric vision (cosmos plus theos, 'divine', plus Andros, 'man'). Monotheism is the matrix of monocentrism, of the intolerance of any other, the establishment of The Only One and the conquest of alterity.

(8)   Realization (*sadhana*) is to visualize the harmony between man's spirit and the divine spirit of the universe, in the living growth of nature. It is a sublime quest of the Infinite. It is a 'rising' towards higher and nobler freedom of consciousness. In Realization, man ascends into a luminous vision of perfection, while in Revelation he has to accede to imperatives. There are no pagans, no infidels in sadhana or Realization. While in Revelation man is in the image of God, in Realization gods are in the image of Man. The human ascent to the Divine, and not a Divine condescension through a book. Sadhana is visualization, contemplation, luminosity growing from within. Sadhana is an epiphany of the divine in human consciousness. In the words of the Rig Veda, it is to find the bonds of being in Non-being (*sata bandhum asati niravindan*). In the ancient Indo-European world, realization was central to human transcension, as distinct from revelation in the Judeocentric tradition. Revelation, on the one hand, is a communication to a lesser mind and demands unquestioning acceptance. Realization or sadhana, on the other hand, is a visualization of truth, a cultivation by meditation, a transfiguration of the individual into the majesty of the Divine. Epic moments of human life are fragments of Divine splendour. As the Bhagavad Gita says: *yad-yad vibhutimat sattvam, srimad urjitam eva val tad-tad evavagaccha tvam, mama tejo-msa-sambhavam/I*, 'the universe is animated by an all-pervading divine radiation: wherever this current attains a particular intensity, a higher

voltage, revealing itself as beauty, power, wonder, there the Supreme becomes apparent, there is the Divine.'

(9) Non-acquisiton (*aparigraha*). The real fulfilment of the human spirit is that values of the inner life mitigate the acid rain of unbridled pursuit of material wealth. Continued industrial exploitation will invite massive retaliation by nature. Man has to give up the illusion of being the supreme creation, whose mission has a struggle against the forces of nature. He has to be a gentle disciple of life, for the stiff and unbending is the disciple of death. He has to celebrate the green plants that are tender and filled with sap. No universalistic hegemony, no depersonalizing, no voracious bureaucracies. An energizing vision alone can lead to fulfilment. The concept of 'standards of life', promiscuity on the television networks, the glorification of violence, the denial of roots in an unprincipled universalism are leading to the break-up of the family, bizarre crimes by children, the destruction of nature, etc., in a mad race for consumerism. For normalization of life, for the renewal of our inner space and to avoid deracination in multipolar societies, we need to give up unnecessary acquisitions, to inculcate a vision of values as the supreme quest of life, to bring about a world wherein the state of Being overrides the plenty of possession. This has to be a 'Century of Life' that will preserve the inside against the outside. 'Creative Coexistence' and 'Autonomy of Will' have to become the absorption of the human mind and action. 'Spiritual ideals of reciprocity' have to shape the heartwork of culture. A new morphology of society will be in consonance with the cosmos, the divine and the human. The quest is not a 'human universal', an offshoot of monotheism, but a 'human harmony' wherein multiple minds and cultural milieus can turn the dynamics of history into the motive power of life. Just as day time fades into night time, so in the world of experience values and life merge. As eternal and universal, it is shaped over the ages, sometimes even after a hiatus of centuries.

Humanity has to move away from glorifying consumerism, sex and violence. The sky looks blue but does not leave its stains on the wings of a bird. To avoid tensions and reprisals, clashes and crashings, the disinherited of the earth will have to be respected and owned. The roots of humanity as a whole must go deep down into the universal and infinite. The series of opposites in creation, negative and positive, assert that the world is a reconciliation of opposing forces. They return in a rhythm, in harmony. The Upanishadic seers having become men-in-the-universe, were inspired by the mighty living cathedrals of nature, and felt that the same serene depths of the mind pulsate in every living being and called upon us to strive for a profound reverence for life:

> Everything has sprung from immoral life
> And is vibrating with life.
> Life is immense.

The value of a simple life has to replace the cult of the consumer. We have to find points of contact with our natural origins. We cannot take goodness and return poison. In the words of Mahatma Gandhi: "I make bold to say that the Europeans will have to remodel their outlook, if they are not to perish under the weight of the comforts to which they are becoming slaves" (Young India 1931).

(10) Confluence of multiple traditions. The emerging world of this century brings humankind closer to each other externally, but a deeper understanding will have to surface to own and honour indefinite number of other cultures and religions.

The humanization of philosophy has to start from the ground of multiple human circumstances to generate plurality. We have to share *shunyata* so that mirages are transformed into visions. From the insignificant nothing of tiny seeds the whole forest is born. The confluence of the nobility of several traditions, functioning in their respective domains, can ensure a harmony of Life, Nature and Enlightenment from the beyond within. To quote Poet Tagore, "every moment it comes from the heart of the master, it is breathed in his breath".

Frontiers create barriers in human understanding. A holy domain, rooted in the immutable word, worked out in painstaking detail in theological structures, breeds a closed sacrum, which has to be defended with all one's might. It cannot but own the vitality of violence. Instead of frontiers, our century needs open horizons, where people are 'sculptors of themselves', to invoke the light and lyricism that lives in our life. As Lalleshvari the great poetess of Kashmir says: "From the outward enter into the most inward part of thy being." The beyond and the within has to be a confluence.

NOTE AND REFERENCE

1. David Hilbert, 1902. *Bulletin of the American Mathematical Society*, 8: 437f.

4

Vedic Tradition and Civilization

N. Kazanas

WHAT IS CIVILIZATION OR CULTURE?

There are many definitions and descriptions in the learned publications.[1]

Here I take 'culture' as synonymous with 'civilization' and in some places with 'tradition', although I am well aware that these terms have different meanings. Etymologically, 'civilization' goes back to the Latin *civis* and *civitas* which indicate life in organized cities which had law and order in contrast to barbarians whose behaviour had little order and much rapacity.

Most think of technology, buildings, artefacts, weapons, etc.

What do we mean today when we say that somebody is 'civilized' or 'cultured'?

We deem 'civilized' those people that are not violent, rapacious and selfish; those that have civility, a broader education and finer valuation of things and take into account the fact that other people also exist and treat them with due consideration. Cultured people are much the same but have also wider interests in the history of mankind, in other nations and in the arts—poetry, painting, music, etc. These are internal qualities and have little to do with large buildings, artefacts and weapons of war that help archaeologists define cultures and civilizations. Thus, from this viewpoint culture and civilization are inner, psychological dispositions that come with inborn goodness and with education and training: they are concerned with one's own refinement and one's behaviour towards other people and towards the environment in which we all live.

In his *Republic* (370C ff.), Plato delineates his first ideal society as a community with simple agriculture, animal husbandry, trade an[d] essential crafts, feeding on barley-bread and bulbs, drinking wine in moderation and singing hymns to the gods.

> *Yoshinory Yasuda on the Japanese Jōmon (11th millennium BCE):*
>
> "Respect for and co-existence with nature ... proper relationship in accord with the features of the given region."
> *A. West on Ancient Egypt* : "In civilization men are concerned with ... inner life ... to master greed, ambition, envy."[2]

From this point of view, modern nations are uncivilized since they do not seek a workable relation with the environment but strive constantly to 'master', as they think, nature and in the process they deplete the planet's resources and cause deadly pollution. In this, there is no concern at all to master greed, ambition and envy.

Yet this is the primary concern of the Vedic tradition: in mastering greed and living harmoniously with one's natural and social environment, one discovers one's true self which is the same as the universal self.

THE RIG VEDIC CULTURE

The Rig Vedic culture is non-material, unlike the Maltese of the fifth millennium with its megalithic temples or the Mesopotamian of the early third millennium with its ziggurats and the parallel Egyptian with it[s] pyramids. The Indus-Sarasvatī Civilization (or Harappan) has buildings, statuary and many artefacts (tools and seals), but the Vedic tradition is oral and this continues down to the Upanishads, the sūtra texts and the epics. What is the axis of this tradition?

> Desire for happiness, health, wealth and heaven. But beneath:
>
> Axis of Vedic culture: 'divinization' or Self-realisation:
> *aham brahma-asmi* (*Bṛh* Up 1.4.10) &

yas tu sarvāṇi bhūtāny-ātmany-eva-anupaśyati /
sarvabhūteṣu ca-ātmānam (Īśā Up 6).

The main concern seems to be divinization, though this appears in the guises of desire for happiness, health, riches on earth or immortality in heaven. Underlying such desires is the knowledge that man embodies the Supreme and that he can realize this. This is plain in the Upanishads with the *mahāvākyas*, 'this Self is Spirit Absolute', *ayam ātmā brahma* and 'I am the brahman', *aham brahma-asmi*. What is not so well known is that this same knowledge is in the *Ṛgveda* too. Yet, consider two statements:

RV 1.164.25: *inó víśvasya bhúvanasya gopāḥ* *sá mā dhīraḥ pākam atrā́ viveśa*	The mighty Guardian of this entire world, He, the wise One has settled in me, the simpleton.
RV 8.6.10: *ahám íd dhí pitús pári medhā́m ṛtásya* *jagrábha ;* *ahám sū́rya iva-ajani.*	Kaṇva says: 'Having received from my father/teacher the essential knowledge (*medhā*) of the Cosmic Order (*ṛta*) I was (re)born like the Sungod *Sūrya*!'

In these two statements, the seer's certain knowledge that the Supreme dwells within him and Kaṇva's realization of a second birth, we see the very basis of the later Vedanta Advaita. And it is to this aspect that most Western people turn to—this and similar aspects of Buddhism. Very few people are drawn to polytheism.

> This 'divinization' *ātmajñāna* or *brahmavidyā*, is achieved through ethical behaviour (*dharma, sukṛtāni, dāna*), yoga-practice and Soma-drinking.
> In *RV* : the One *tad-ekam* (10.129.2).
> Also 1.164.16,46; 3.54.8; 8.58.2.
> Also – Many deities, worlds, phenomena.
> One and Many – synchronically.
> Most interest shown in the Many, less in the One!

But we should note that this most ancient culture had, apart from this higher spiritual concern, also interest and knowledge of the subtle world of mind and of the material world. Long long before Socrates and the other Greek philosophers, the Vedic seers displayed a high level of abstract thought with concepts like *anumati, asuratva, dāna, paṅkti*, etc.

D1

Spiritual concern:	Self-realization; devotion to divinities.
Mental level:	*anumati* *asuratva* *dāna* *paṅkti*
	agreement lordship; liberality; fiveness (also 'row')
	vasutā 'wealthiness'
	Mathematics: algebra, geometry
	Complex grammar: *dhātus* and derivative nouns and verbs with many tenses and moods
	Measure and rhythm in poetry and music
Material world:	Astronomy: constellations and calendar
	Geometry (Śulbasūtras) in building Harappan cities and altars
	Medicine with herbs and mineral substances
	Chanting of hymns; dancing
	Weaving, metallurgy, pottery and other crafts (household utensils and weapons like bows)
	Agriculture and animal husbandry
	Trade with ocean-going boats

Of major importance are the Śulbasūtras of Āpastamba, Āśvalāyana, Kātyāyana and Baudhāyana. These formulate principles of mathematics.

Śulbasūtras

Forming part of the Śrauta Sūtras (Āpastamba, Āśvalāyana, Kātyāyana, Baudhāyana), they belong to the Kalpa Sūtras which are one of the six Vedāṅgas (= 'limbs of Veda').

What is their date?

And one modern authority, A. Seidenberg, American mathematician and historian of science, has written:

> It is very difficult to derive "the Vedic ritual application of the theorem [of Pythagoras] from Babylonia. (The reverse process is easy.) ... The application involves geometric algebra and there is no evidence of

geometric algebra from Babylonia. And the geometry of Babylonia is already secondary whereas in India it is primary. Hence we do not hesitate to place the Vedic altar rituals, or, more exactly, rituals exactly like them, far back of 1700 BCE.... The elements of ancient geometry found in Egypt and Babylonia stem from a ritual system of the kind observed in the Sulvasutras".[3]

Seidenberg reiterated his finds in another paper in 1978.

Note that the Mesopotamian ziggurats (= temples with steps) and the Egyptian mastamba tombs and the step pyramid of Djoser, all in the third millennium BCE, are based on trapezoid figures which are found in the Śulbasūtras and those figures are at the basis of Vedic altar brick-constructions like the śmaśana-cit.

Thus, latest date for Śulbasūtras must be c. 2600 BCE.

Figure 4.1: Trapezoid Figures found in the Śulbas and in Egypt and Mesopotamia

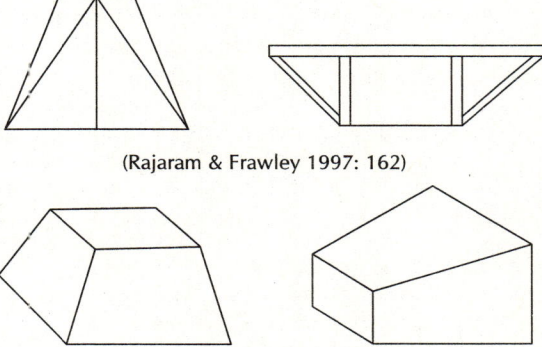

(Rajaram & Frawley 1997: 162)

The Egyptian *mastaba* (left) and the Vedic śmaśāna-cit altar
(Rajaram & Frawley 1997: 162)

Source: Created by Dr Frawley and Rajaram.

Foundations of linguistic studies:
Yāska (*Nighaṇṭu* & *Nirukta*);
Pāṇini (*Aṣṭādhyāyī*).
Concepts (of *Vibhakti* and) *kāraka* in West only in 19th cent. – i.e. surface and deep structure grammar and meaning.

After internecine wars some people
are scattered far over the earth (*abhí kṣā́m* 7.18.16)
and some pushed to the West *(... pūrváś cakāra áparām ... 7.6.3)*.

10.65.11 : *sū́ryaṃ diví roháyantaḥ nava sudā āryā vratā visṛjánto ádhi kṣami*
'the bounteous gods made the sun mount in heaven and diversely released
(*vi-sṛj-*) the Aryan laws over the earth'.

VEDIC TRADITION IN THE NEAR EAST

(1) *c. 3000, Possible Influence on Egypt—Affinities in Religion*: Creation
     through speech; sungod's boat; cow of plenty; lotus-born one;
     creator's eye running off and being brought back; etc.[4]
     Also, the Śulbasūtra geometry and trapezoids for mastaba
     tombs and step pyramid, etc.[5]

(2) *c. 2600 on Mesopotamia*: Actual trade links. Affinities in religion:
     seven ṛṣis; flood legend; horse sacrifice; magical rituals; etc.[6]
     Also the Śulbasūtra geometry and ziggurats.[7]

(3) Perhaps Judaic culture with monotheism.[8]

Kassites & Mitannis in the Near East (17th-16th centuries BCE).
Apart from Indoaryan names and horse-husbandry, under Agum II in early
16th cent. – "A surge of literacy invention, collection and recording"[9]
A rennaissance with – perhaps – ideas of Vedic origin.

Unity of Being in 1st & 2nd cent. CE:
Hermeticists and Christian Gnostics 1st & 2nd cent.
Neoplatonists and Neopythagoreans 3rd cent.
(*Enneads* of Plotinos; Porphyry; Iamblichos).
Influence of Vedic Tradition (?)

This doctrine of the Unity of Being, of Man and Cosmos must have
come from the Vedic tradition of India.[10] Plotinus' teaching reflects most
faithfully Advaita: there is only the One without a second and from his
gaze or consciousness out of love and bliss arises the creation; first comes
Nous (= higher mind or reason) which as creative cause brings all else
into existence with the power from the One, then comes the level of Soul
(= subtle world, *sūkṣma śarira*) and finally the material embodiments of
worlds and creatures. Man can and should strive through self-knowledge
to return and merge in the primal unity of the One.

Perhaps some influence after Persian conquests in 6th cent BCE. Certainly there were translations of literature 5th cent CE (some of these tales reached Syria in the NE).

Also translation of 50 Upanishads in seventeenth century CE under Prince Mohammed Dara Shakoh.

Figure 4.2: Sanskrit, Hinduism and Buddhism in Asia

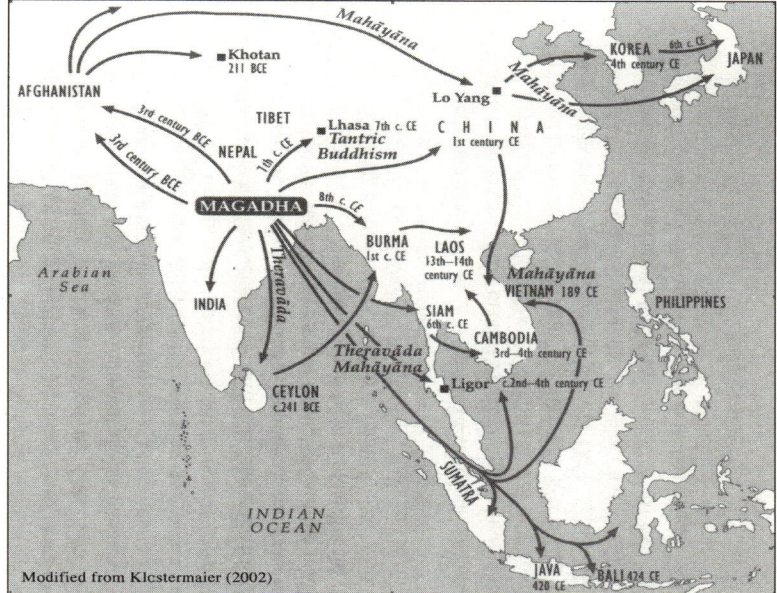

Source: Created by Dr Klostermaier.

Sanskrit vocabulary in South East Asia

argha > *haliga/harga* 'price';
kāya > *kāya* 'body';
buddhi > *buḍhi/budi* 'inclination/character'.
aṅgula 'finger', *āyus* 'life', *gaja* 'elephant'
jala 'water', *dāna* 'charity, gift', *velā* 'limit', etc.

Buddhism spread South in the late centuries BCE. It was established fully in Shri Lanka and later spread eastward into Indonesia, Laos and other areas of South East Asia. Hinduism also spread later. Sanskrit accompanied both religions. So, although other influences came later in the Common Era with Muslims and Christians and European languages, Spanish, Portuguese, English and Dutch, nonetheless, even today many words of Sanskrit origin survive in the languages and dialects spoken in those communities. Thus in Tagalok: *balita*, 'tidings', from *vṛtta*, 'what has occurred, news'; *buḍhi*, 'inclination', from *buddhi*, 'higher intellect'; *basa*, 'reading out', from *vāca*, 'recitation'; *halaga*, 'price', from *argha*, 'price', etc. In Malay: *budi*, 'character', again from *buddhi* and *harga*, 'price', from *argha*. Also, *kaca*, 'glass', from *kāca*, 'crystal, glass'; *puasa*, 'fast', from *uparāsa*, 'fast'; *kāya*, 'body', from *kāya*, 'body', etc. In other languages, Thai, Lao, Cambodian, etc., survive *aṅgula*, 'finger'; *āgama*, 'religion'; *āyus*, 'life'; *gaja*, 'elephant'; *gaṇa*, 'group'; *jala*, 'water'; *jāla*, 'net'; *tarā*, 'star'; *dāna*, 'gift, charity'; *bhāṣā*, 'language'; *velā*, 'limit'; etc.[11]

Buddhism spread northward as well into what is today Afghanistan, then Tibet and China, and Sanskrit again accompanied the religion. It entered into China in the reign of Emperor Ming Ti (58–76 CE) with Indian monks. The missionary activities of these Buddhist monks in south-western China drew the attention of aristocrats and intellectuals by the end of the first century CE. A poem by Chang Heng survives from this period (75–100 CE) mentioning virtuous *shramana*s, that is, Buddhist monks. But the linguistic impact of Sanskrit was as important as the theology of Buddhism. In the late third century, an Indian monk, Mokṣala, introduced into Chinese writing 42 *siddham* letters, that is, modified Brahmī characters that would help change the Chinese ideogrammatic script and later pass into Japan as well. Thus, eventually, Sanskrit helped reform the Chinese writing system and its phonetics. In the fourth century, Sanskrit became much better known (both its writing and phonology); but its highly inflectional grammar remained prohibitive for the Chinese who were thoroughly habituated to their own isolating language—wherein every individual morpheme or sound was a meaningful word—so Sanskrit never gained a foothold in China. But translations of texts began to appear in the fifth century: Dharmakṣema, another Indian *shramana*, first translated into Chinese the *Mahāparinirvāṇa Sūtra*; such translations multiplied in the ensuing centuries. From the eighth century in China survives in a fragment the oldest extant 'printed' mantras for Goddess Pratisarā, while from the ninth century survives the oldest extant printed book which is the *Vajracchedikā Sūtra*. Thus, paper prints in Sanskrit are far older in China than in India! In 526 Bodhidharma, the Patriarch of Indian Buddhism (twenty-eighth successor to Buddha) had migrated to China.[12]

In the fourth century, Buddhism reached Korea, again through zealous missionary activity.[13]

In the middle of the sixth century, Buddhism and Sanskrit entered into Japan. The powerful Prince Shotoko Taishi recognized that some of the doctrines of the new religion had transcendental values and provided a basis for unity and integrity, particularly with the popular ideas *bahujana-hitāya*, 'for the good of many', and *bahujana-sukhāya*, 'for the happiness of many'; so he drew up the first Constitution in Japan with 17 articles having as a fundamental factor the Buddhist *tri-ratna*, 'three jewels'—Buddha, dharma and *saṅga*. He also wrote commentaries on several sūtras like *Sad-dharma-pundarīke*, etc. Three hundred years later, c. 850, King Shomu dispatched Sanskrit Buddhist Sūtras to the provinces and ordered that they be recited on fixed days and times, thereby creating strong unity in the whole country. A little later, under Empress Shotoku, several texts were printed and thereafter many more. In the early ninth century, the system of education opened out to more classes of people while the monk-scholar Kobo Daishi, under the guidance of the Kashmiri scholar Prajña, created new alphabet(s) based on the Nāgarī script and called Shittan (a corruption of *siddham*). Here also, we see not only religious but also a political and a linguistic impact—which, of course, continued in Japan in subsequent centuries.[14]

In the seventh century, Buddhism became the creed of Tibet under the influence of its ruler Srong Tsan Gambo. He himself was influenced by his two wives: one was a princess of the Chinese royal house and the other Nepalese. This king also united the country under his sway. Later many monasteries were established and to these found refuge thousands of monks when the Muslims invaded India and destroyed the northern cities Nalanda and Taxila.

VEDIC INFLUENCES IN THE WEST

More recently, after the British discovered Sanskrit literature, literary and philosophical ideas came to Europe and America in the late eighteenth century and early nineteenth century (for example, Emerson in the

US, Schopenhauer in Germany and Eliot in Britain). With Sanskrit, linguistic studies took on new form, intensity and direction. But new stronger influences began to spread in the late nineteenth century when various sages travelled to Europe and the USA bringing the teaching of Vedānta. Many more came to the West in the twentieth century. I shall confine myself only to the mention of the poet T.S. Eliot who quoted in his *Wasteland*, end, the *Bṛhadāranyaka Upanishad* (5.2.1 ff.), *dāmyata*, 'restrain yourselves', gods; *datta*, 'be generous', men; *dayadhvam*, 'be compassionate', demons. Eliot also cited the *Bhāgavad Gītā* in his *Four Quartets*, even though he was a Christian with leanings towards Catholicism.

Exports to the West from 19th cent. onward :
Literature and Linguistic ideas;
(e.g. Emerson in the USA, Schopenhauer in Germany, Eliot in Britain;)
Vedānta and Buddhism;
Āyurveda, Meditation and Yoga

Beyond these, India has exported to the West and the whole world three great items: *āyurveda*, various forms of meditation, and, of course, yoga, which is probably the best known one. But this is the grossest form of yoga, *Haṭha-yoga*, with its taxing *āsana*s. The basic, the real yoga of Patañjali, has eight limbs or stages.

Astāṅga-yoga of Patañjali (2.29)
Eight Stages (Limbs) of Yoga

8) samādhi	Absorption
7) dhyāna	Meditation
6) dhāraṇā	Concentration of the Mind
5) pratyāhāra	Withdrawal of the Senses
4) prāṇāyāma	Breath Regulation
3) āsana	Body Position
2) niyama	Internal Rules
1) yama	External Rules (Code of Conduct)

Patañjali's yoga is designed to reduce and stop the movements in the mind:

yogaś citta-vṛtti-nirodha (1.2)
Yoga effects the cessation of mind-movements.

All such movements of thinking and feeling are caused, says Patañjali, by five *kleśas*.

5 kleśas 'afflictions' (2.3)

avidyā	*Asmitā*	*rāga*	*dveṣa*	*abhiniveśa*
ignorance	egoism (separate ego)	attachment, passion	abhorence	attachment to the world

To harness and dissolve these malignant tendencies, Patañjali prescribed several disciplines. In regard to *āsanas*, 'positions', he says only that the *asana* should be *sthira sukha*, 'steady and easy'! That is all—nothing more. But he says a lot on other practices like *dhāraṇā*, 'concentration', *dhyāna*, 'meditation', etc.

One starts with *yama*, Stage 1. There are five *yamas*, that is, five regulations for external behaviour:

Five regulations (yamas) (2.30)

ahiṃsā	*satya*	*asteya*	*brahmacarya*	*aparigraha*
non-injury	truth	non-stealing	life of purity	non-grabbing, non-amassing

The last one is the key. It implies control of desire. When one does not desire more than one needs, then there will not be stealing, lying and injuring others and life will be simple and pure. If *parigraha*, desire, and grabbing and amassing all around motivates us, then egoism, *asmitā*, and the other *kleśas* with ambition, envy and greed will grow and produce all the evils of our society.

'GIVING': THE VIRTUE OF THIS AGE

The positive virtue to the *aparigraha* is *dāna*, generosity. Plato's and Justinian's definition of justice is 'giving to everyone what is due'. From the *Ṛgveda* the ancient seers praised generosity or liberality (*Ṛgveda*).

Ṛgveda 10.117	*Hymn to Generosity*
Bṛhadāraṇyaka Up	*datta '[humans], give'!*
Manusmṛti 1.86	*dānam ekaṃ kalau yuge*
	'giving alone in the kali yuga'
Bhagavad Gītā	8.28; 16.1; etc.

We live in the Kali Yuga which is the worst epoch and in which dharma is reduced at its lowest. We saw in the last century genocides, tortures and killings on a massive scale perpetrated by totalitarian regimes like these of Stalin and Hitler, while terrorism continues on all continents of the planet. Events such as these have never happened before in recorded human history.

DESCENT INTO DEGRADATION

In our own Age, the Kali Yuga, the ancient teachings have been pushed aside or have been wholly forgotten. We see around ever-mounting greed for increasing profits and easy pleasures—all quick and with as little responsibility as possible. The feverish acquisition of material wealth is to secure power and the indulgence of selfish desires. This has two powerful global effects. One is the degradation and weakening of man's natural abilities. The other is the plundering and denudation of the planet's natural resources resulting in the deadly environment pollution.

Starting with the second, the degradation of the natural environment, we all know of the hot-house effects as pollution increases globally—not only in India—from industrial sewage, fumes out of factories and vehicles, chemical fertilizers, insecticides, sprays of everykind, etc.

One glaring example in India is the depletion and pollution of Ganges, felt most acutely at Kanpur and Allahabad. By the time the river reaches Varanasi, other tributaries do provide fresh amounts of cleaner water. Even so, in the region of Varanasi, although some decades ago the Ganges had an average depth of 60 metres, now it has only 10 and in some spots it almost disappears, especially just before the river meets the Yamuna before Allahabad. (So an article by Jyoti Thottam in the *Time* magazine, 19 July 2010.) First, the glaciers up in the Himalayas diminish as part of the general course whereby the perennial ices in the Arctic and Antarctic gradually melt. Second, the Tehri Dam above Rishikesh diverts waters from key tributaries of the Ganges. Third, the explosive uncontrolled growth of cities (like Delhi and Kanpur) and of agriculture draw increased amounts of water while city-sewers and industries (like the Kanpur tanneries) return only wastewater and toxins.

D2

Depletion and pollution of Ganges waters

    Himalaya glaciers diminish

    Tehri Dam absorbs tributaries

    Increasing canals for supplying agriculture and cities

    Uncontrolled, explosive growth of cities

    City sewage and industrial toxins into the river

    Drop of average level at Varanasi from 60 down to 10 metres

Other problems:

    Caste system, cruelty to girls and widows

    Increasing gap between rich and poor

Other problems are the caste system which condemns millions into poverty and other unfavourable conditions, the cruel treatment of young girls and millions of ill-starred widows and, generally, the increase in the gap between rich and poor or privileged and underprivileged. This is the modern face of India which has many deepening wrinkles from the past and the heavy make-up of the present as it assumes the looks of the West. But now let us look at the attrition of man's innate powers.

Studies in 2002 reveal that:

$$
\text{In Germany, youngsters could before 1970 distinguish} < \begin{cases} 350 \text{ colours} \\ 300{,}000 \text{ sounds} \end{cases}
$$

$$
\text{today only} < \begin{cases} 130 \text{ colours} \\ 180{,}000 \text{ sounds} \end{cases}
$$

In France and USA, youngsters had vocabulary   25,000 words

today only 10,000 words

Let me give you some statistics from the year 2002. In Germany, child development studies (in Tübingen University) revealed that while before 1970, young people could distinguish about 300,000 sounds, now many cannot go beyond 100,000 and the average is 180,000; while they could detect 350 different shades of one colour, today the number is 130.[15]

Other studies in the USA and France showed that children in underdeveloped countries or primitive rural settings averaged an awareness of their surroundings 25–30 per cent higher than children of technologically developed countries.[16] Then, American high school students of 1950 had a working vocabulary of some 25,000 words; today they have only 10,000. Moreover, there was an increase of over one million of daily doses of different drugs that alter children's behaviour.[17] These few selected facts confirm that Kali Yuga cascades downward at great speed.

From most ancient times we hear that greed in the frame of ignorance is the root of all evils. So the sages, prophets and saints in all cultures stressed the need to restrain it. In the Ṛgveda, there is a whole hymn on liberality dakṣiṇā (Ṛgveda 10 117). The Bṛhadāraṇyaka Upanishad says datta, 'give!' (5.2.2). The Taittirīya Up commands that a householder should always prepare food and never drive anyone away. And the Manusmṛti declares explicitly that the virtue in the Kali Yuga is dāna, 'giving' (dānam ekaṃ kalau yuge). Greeks and Romans said that justice is giving to all their due. Christ too exhorts his followers—'Give and it shall be given to you' (Luke 6.38). Giving, giving, giving. And of course the fifth regulation in aṣṭāṅga yoga is aparigraha, 'not coveting, not grabbing from all around'!

Despite the obvious spiralling down of Kali Yuga, a renaissance is possible just as it was realized several times in the past both in the East and the West. But first, the times must be right and ripe: there must be some measure of peace and prosperity in society. Then a decisive group of dedicated people must work in a disciplined way for this. A third factor is the influx of new knowledge that brings about a radical change of mind and heart in people so that they meet the practical problems of the daily routine in a new way. I have found these three factors operating in every flowering of renaissance.

I think the Vedic tradition could perform its miracle again. It was based on oral tradition not the visual kaleidoscopic impressions of our modern culture; not so much the eye but the ear led to understanding. We must learn to listen again. The study of Advaita, the practice of meditation and the application of the five *yama*s in daily life for the sake of all people could produce good results.

Five regulations (yamas) (2.30)

ahiṃsā	*satya*	*asteya*	*brahmacarya*	*aparigraha*
non-injury	truth	non-stealing	life of purity	non-grabbing, non-amassing

Yoshinory Yasuda on the Japanese Jōmon (eleventh millennium BCE):

> "Respect for and co-existence with nature … proper relationship in accord with the features of the given region."
> *A. West on Ancient Egypt* : "In civilization men are concerned with … inner life … to master greed, ambition, envy."[18]

NOTES AND REFERENCES

1. See S. Bhattacharya, 'Theories of the Nature of Civilization', in G.C. Pande (ed.), *Golden Chain of Civilizations* (Delhi and Simla: Centre for Studies in Civilizations, 2007), 111–31; L. Kramer and S. Maza, *A Companion to Western Historical Thought* (Oxford: Blackwell, 2002); J.C. Pearce, *The Biology of Transcendence* (Rochester:

Vermont Park Street Press, 2002); W. Schafer, 'Global Civilization', *International Sociology* 16, no. 3 (2001): 304–11; R. Williams, *Keywords: A Vocabulary of Culture* (NY, Oxford: Oxford University Press, 1991); L. White, *A Science of Culture: A Study of Man Civilization* (NY: Noonday Press, 1969).

2. For Yasuda, see Rudgley, *Lost Civilizations of the Stone Age* (Londom: Century, 1998), 31–33. Also see A. West's publication of 1993, pages 6–7.

3. A. Seidenberg, 'The Ritual Origin of Geometry', Archive for History of the Exact Sciences 1 (1962): 488–527. The findings are reproduced in A. Seidenberg, 'The Origin of Mathematics', in *Archive for History of the Exact Sciences* 18 (1978): 301–42.

4. N. Kazanas, *Indo Aryan Origins and Other Vedic Issues* (Delhi: Aditya Prakashan, 2009), Chapter 8.

5. N. Rajaram and D. Frawley, *Vedic Aryans & Origins of Civilisation* (Delhi: Voice of India, 1997).

6. N. Kazanas, *Indo Aryan Origins and Other Vedic Issues*, Chapter 7.

7. N. Rajaram and D. Frawley, *Vedic Aryans & Origins of Civilisation*.

8. N. Kazanas, *Indo Aryan Origins and Other Vedic Issues*, Chapter 7.

9. S. Dalley, *Myths from Mesopotamia* (Oxford: Oxford University Press, 1991), 47, 299.

10. N. Kazanas, 'Advaita & Gnosticism', *VVRI Research Bulletin* 2 (2003).

11. J. Gonda, 'Sanskrit in Indonesia', in Sh. Kumar (ed.), *Sanskrit across Cultures* (New Delhi: Printworld Ltd, 2007), 139–70.

12. Chaudhuri, 'Sanskrit in China', in Sh. Kumar (ed.), *Sanskrit across Cultures* (New Delhi: Printworld Ltd, 2007), 7–36; K. Klostermaier, *Buddhism* (Oxford: Oneworld Publications, 2002 [1999]); J. Yasuda, 'The Changing Aristocratic Society', *Acta Asiatica* 60 (Tokyo: 1991); K. Ch'en, *Buddhism in China* (Princeton: Princeton University Press, 1973); W. Soothill, *The Three Religions of China* (London: Curzon: 1973 [1929]).

13. Klostermaier, *Buddhism*.

14. Shashibala, 'Sanskrit in Japan', in Sh. Kumar (ed.), *Sanskrit across Cultures* (New Delhi: Printworld Ltd, 2007), 37–62; E. Conze, *A Short History of Buddhism* (Oxford: Oneworld Publications, 1993).

15. J.C. Pearce, *The Biology of Transcendence*, 111.

16. J.C. Pearce, *The Biology of Transcendence*, 112.

17. J.C. Pearce, *The Biology of Transcendence*, 113.

18. For Yasuda, see Rudgley, *Lost Civilizations of the Stone Age*, 31–33. Also see A. West's publication of 1993, pages 6–7.

5

On Three Images of India

Balmiki Prasad Singh

I

Every person likes to comment about India even if he or she has never lived in or even visited this country once. And those who have lived in the country do not entertain one idea. They give expression to conflicting thoughts. Either they love it or hate it. Similarly, in the corpus of literature, the Indian image has been described in manifold ways ranging from sublime to the ridiculous.

I would, however, confine myself to three dominant images of India in view of their importance as well as relevance both to us Indians and to the modern world. These are: (*a*) the Indian approach to the life of spirit and the matter; (*b*) India's secular democracy in a plural society; and (*c*) the Bahudha approach of social harmony and conflict resolution.

II

Mahatma Gandhi, more than anybody else in India's contemporary history, provided an image of India both before his people and to the wider world. The cornerstone of this image is based on principles of truth and non-violence, which have been enunciated from the days of Lord Mahavira and Lord Gautama Buddha. In the context of epic struggle for India's freedom, Bapu's concept of satyagraha not only empowered common people but also helped generate in them a sense of fearlessness. The most important aspect of the India's image, however, which Bapu both preached and practiced, was of simple living and attachment to high ideals. This was the way Bapu handled the matter of spirit and the material world.

In August this year I had the privilege of visiting Sevagram Ashram, which was Bapu's home between 1934 and 1947. It may be recalled that Mahatma Gandhi on return from South Africa set up the famous Sabarmati Ashram in Ahmedabad in 1917. A few days before the launch of Salt Satyagraha on 12 March 1930, Bapu mentioned to Ba that he was getting attached to Sabarmati Ashram, which was in conflict with ideals of non-attachment. Ba immediately understood that Bapu would give up the ashram and that they would be again homeless.

On the eve of the Salt March, Bapu announced that he will not come back to Sabarmati Ashram till India gets independence. On completion of the Salt March on 6 April 1930, Ba and Bapu had no house of their own.

Seth Jamnalal Bajaj, a prominent disciple of Bapu, was deeply concerned and succeeded in persuading Bapu to set up an ashram at Wardha where he owned lot of land. Bapu visited the place and approved the site. He, however, put a condition that not more than ₹500 shall be spent on the construction of his hut and that it shall be built by materials available locally. Adi Ashram was accordingly raised. Bapu lived here for over 10 years without electricity and on two simple vegetarian meals. None of us would like to spend even seven days in such a place!

The image of austere living and attachment to high values that this ashram generated and continues to do so is in consonance with the living conditions of the people of India and also our heritage. As Rabindranath Tagore said: "Gandhiji sat at the thresholds of the huts of the thousands of dispossessed, dressed like one for their own. He spoke to them in their own language."[1]

The common people of India too have in their day-to-day lives promoted spiritual values living austerely. The Indian watchers in Western countries have always been impressed by the metaphysical bent of Indian minds and at times they have wondered whether the Indians are dreamers. But this is not the correct position. Spirituality is a strong feature of the Indian mind but India saw from the very beginning both in her ages of prosperity and in her years of decline that the ideal way of living would need a judicious combination of both material and spiritual values. As Sri Aurobindo rightly said:

[L]ife cannot be rightly seen in the sole light, cannot be perfectly lived in the sole power of its externalities. She was alive to the greatness of material laws and forces; she had a keen eye for the importance of the physical sciences; she knew how to organize the arts of ordinary life. But she saw that the physical does not get its full sense until it stands in right relations to the supra-physical.[2]

In the present era of globalization and integration of markets, the lifestyle of people is changing dramatically. We are rapidly adopting conspicuous consumption norms and displaying our wealth. The unrestrained consumption currently indulged in by the middle class in India may over the years create a counter image of 'self-indulgent Indians'. Would Indians be completely won over by Western consumption norms? Would the Lokayukta school of Canvaka that advocated the good life prevail over Buddha and Gandhi? I hope not.

III

The second image of India is of secular democracy.

It may be recalled that during 1945–1960, about 100 countries got independence from the colonial rule. Several of these countries were torn by civil wars. Rulers in many newly liberated countries became autocrats but India stood apart and persisted with democracy based on principles of pluralism and secularism notwithstanding the partition of India into India and Pakistan based on religion.

The universal adult suffrage, equality of every citizen irrespective of class, caste and gender; free and fair elections; a free press; an independent judiciary; and a culture of liberal thought have unleashed forces that have imparted a degree of robustness to Indian democracy. It has generated clamour for good governance and strengthened forces of social harmony. The establishment of high-quality technological and educational institutions, a sizeable middle class and information society have provided vigour to the Indian democratic system.

It is no wonder that *aam admi* or the common people in India exercise their rights to change the ruling elite both at the centre as well as in the states during elections which have been held regularly as prescribed under the Constitution.

A silent revolution among Indian women is taking place. A vibrant Indian democracy has ensured participation of 1.2 million elected women officials. The Indian economy is being supported by nearly a million active women micro-credit workers and more than half of the workforce in a country of 1 billion people is women.

There can be no one way—religions, caste, culture or linguistic—of being an Indian. Pluralism is the founding principle for building a pan-Indian identity and need not be in conflict with other identities. To accord respect to identity of others is a part of our constitutional obligation.

In today's India, democracy supports inclusiveness (notwithstanding polarization on caste and religious lines) and this would be furthered through education and availability of internet facilities in the major languages of India. This will also mean better governance, a more informed society and market and prosperity for our people.

India's new economic policy has unleashed creative energy of the business class. There is a new emphasis on efficiency, productivity and competition. However, a close look at the components of growth would reveal that it has not only generated gross inequality in income and access to good education and health care but also environmental degradation and corruption.

In this environment, there is need to place considerable stress on integrity as well because the Indian psyche still attaches considerable importance to moral values. That integrity in public life is also linked to efficient and transparent work ethic and deserves to be accorded special attention. The right to information (Right to Information Act, 2005) has emerged as an effective instrument in the hands of the common people to check corruption, fight injustice and make governance transparent.

The right-wing religious fundamentalists and the extreme left seek to redefine the Indian democratic system in terms of their own ideals. If the right wing succeeds, the nature of secular democracy would undergo major transformation. The success of the left-wing extremists would give currency to 'the gun' in the country. Fortunately, these forces lack popular support.

Some people even think that democratic system is noisy, messy and dilatory in handling these challenges. It is, however, our faith that in the long run, democracy alone through people's unity and determination shall prevail over terrorist and fundamentalist forces.

Would the forces of terrorism, left-wing extremism, fundamentalist elements and insurgents succeed in creating a counter image? Would mafia and muscle power succeed in subverting the Indian democracy? The struggle is on.

IV

The third image of India relates to its civilizational experience in the modern world. I have personal journey to narrate in this behalf. This was mentioned by Professor Molly Kaushal in her welcome address.

The rise of terrorism and fundamentalism in the recent times has brought about phenomenal changes in global politics. These unprecedented challenges call for a new, bold and imaginative statecraft from the world leaders. What would be the nature of Indian response?

It was during my tenure as executive director, World Bank, at Washington DC, that the catastrophe of 9/11 took place. In the aftermath of the tragedy, it became fashionable for every think tank to discuss two questions: 'what went wrong?' and 'why people hate us (American)?' I happened to attend one such meeting barely 10 days after the catastrophe. The gathering was impressive; I was seated almost opposite the chairperson. The guest speaker had concluded on the sombre note of the need for building a coalition of nations against terrorism. He also spoke of the radicalization of Islam, values of religious pluralism and the need for tolerance. The presentation over, the chairperson asked for comments and looked at me. She said that India may have the answer in view of its heritage of pluralism and originality of mind, and gave me the floor. I was not prepared. I recall having said then that "while India may have the answer, I do not" and went on to narrate my experiences in handling terrorism in India.

I have been contemplating this theme since then with a view to exploring an enduring framework for global public policy—a policy for harmony among different people and societies in the post 9/11 world as seen through the lens of the Indian experience.

It is said that when the student is ready, the teacher will appear. I was drawn to an attitude that has greatly contributed to the enrichment of Indian life; 'respect for another person's view of truth with hope and belief that he or she may be right', this is best expressed in the Rig Vedic hymn that enjoins:

Ekam Sad Vipra Bahudha Vadanti
The Real is one, the learned speak of it variously.

I imagine this approach of 'one truth, many expressions' was formulated by our rishis both in order to understand the complexities of natural objects and their interrelationships and for harmonious living in society among people of multifarious beliefs and practices.

The Bahudha approach not only underlines equal respect for all points of view but also calls for—and that is significant—inculcation of a habit in which one person thinks that the other person's point of view may perhaps be right. Understanding the point of view of those with whom one profoundly disagrees is the first step towards learning to create a society which manages such disagreement. Such an approach which is a dialogue of harmony and peaceful living thus becomes an imperative in our times.

The Bahudha approach has drawn strength from common people as well as rulers. In our long and uninterrupted civilizational history, one thing strikes us constantly that the common people of India have always provided strength to the values of pluralism and tolerance. It has also been shaped by India's historical experiences.

India has been living through pluralistic challenge longer than several other nations. In terms of faith, well before the advent of Christianity and Islam in the West and other parts of the world, India was significant playfield of civilizational encounters between Hinduism, Buddhism and Jainism. Both Judaism and Christianity came to India in the first century itself. Islam too commenced its entry through the coastal towns of the Indian peninsula from the eighth century onwards. In the ninth century, when the Zoroastrians of Persia felt that their religion was in danger from the invading Muslims, they moved to the north-west coast of India. Their descendants still live there and are known as Parsis. The birth of Sikhism in the fifteenth century in India had the avowed objective of bringing peace to conflicting encounters among Hinduism and Islam. In the last century, when the Tibetans felt a threat to their religion and culture, they chose India as a refuge and a large number of them live here.

Multiculturalism is a basic feature of India's civilizational experience. In its practice in India, it is not atheistic in character but a combination of religions. No wonder India in the past successfully accommodated and assimilated different points of view and in the religious domain in particular created images and institutions for 330 million gods and goddesses.

It is true that India has at different times in history deviated from the Bahudha approach. The partition of India is a case in point. The partition was not only a political failure but also a civilizational failure.

A question is often posed about the role and relevance of the military in the construction of an environment for creative dialogue among civilizations. In the post 9/11 world, it is quite obvious that the ugly face of terrorism has given full justification for a strong military posture. In fact, the rise of terrorist activities indifferent parts of the world demands it. This, however, does not mean that military intervention can be taken in an arbitrary fashion either within the country or among nation states.

In the aftermath of the 26/11 Mumbai tragedy, we have rightly reacted with restraint. We have appropriately moved towards the strengthening of our legal framework, our security infrastructure and our criminal justice system.

Towards inculcation of Bahudha approach, we have to give fresh look at the central role of education in the life of the youth and use religious beliefs of tolerance in the building of harmonious society. It is also necessary to strengthen the United Nations to become an effective global conflict resolution mechanism.

CONCLUSION

Let me conclude. Would these three values of austerity, secular democracy and dialogue of harmony continue to define the image of India? For these three images of India have found relevance in the Indian society in unexpected ways. These could be seen and experienced when we meet people at the fairs or in bazaars or in religious congregations or even in this seminar.

It was Mahatma Gandhi who once said: "The Rich must live more simply so that the Poor may simply live." It is only through secular democracy and dialogue among people that we can nourish the plural society. It is my firm belief that as long as Indian society and polity encourage creative minds in the literature and the arts, science and technology and give primacy to democratic institutions and to our approach of an inclusive and just social order, the three main Indian images that I have outlined before you would continue to characterize us.

NOTES AND REFERENCES

1. Quoted in Rabindranath Tagore, *A Centenary Volume 1861–1961*, XIV.
2. Shri Aurobindo, *The Renaissance in India* (1920), 14.

6

Cross-cultural Conversation and Diplomacy

Shyam Saran

The very raison d'être of the profession I represent, diplomacy, is anchored in cross-cultural engagement. In fact, I would go further and assert that diplomacy is cross-cultural conversation. A diplomat is a *duta* or an envoy. But he is not merely a messenger. He is an interlocutor, whose skills are rooted in an ability to converse in an idiom familiar to his opposite number. This requires a cultivated sensitivity to the cultural particularities of the country to which he is accredited and an ability to sense the changes in moods and expressions, or what is popularly known as body language, for clues to what lies behind formal articulations. There may be occasions when such ability or lack thereof may spell the difference between war and peace. War, in fact, represents the most dramatic and indeed most tragic breakdown of cross-cultural communication, when nations get caught up inexorably in a cumulatively reinforcing vortex of misunderstanding, misperception and suspicion which leads almost inevitably to violence.

To me, successful diplomacy is only possible when there is cultural empathy, irrespective of whether one is dealing with a current adversary or an ally. Cultural empathy begins with that ancient urge of curiosity, a perennial eagerness to explore the unfamiliar and the sense of enrichment which comes from appreciating that the human spirit manifests itself in myriad dazzling forms. There is that sense of wonder at how the genius of a people, strangers to us till yesterday, mirrors our own preoccupations with life and its mysteries, but expressed in ways that surprise and delight us with their novelty.

My own experience has been that in the process of exploring and appreciating another culture, I began to feel the need to know more about my own culture in all its bewildering variety. Then came the urge to share, to expose others to our own cultural heritage, while in the midst of the process of understanding the other. After all, projecting the best that India has to offer, to showcase the Indian spirit in its finest expressions, is what an Indian diplomat is expected to do. He may not be a Gandhian in the values he practices as an individual. The country he represents may not be true to its Gandhian heritage. But in projecting this heritage, he is representing the best his country has to offer and that is of value in itself. A diplomat is the medium for cross-cultural communication, where the best that each has to offer engenders engagement. Each side begins to draw strength and inspiration from the other in a process that may often be invisible and osmotic.

Let me dwell awhile on the power of culture as a facet of diplomacy. The success of Bollywood and the popular culture it represents is, of course, legendary even if it is sniffed at with some disdain by the votaries of high culture. In Indonesia, Shah Rukh Khan is probably better known and certainly more popular than some of the country's top leaders. Indian movie songs are hummed everywhere even if their lyrics are only vaguely understood. When we first arrived in Jakarta in 2001, when I was appointed ambassador, my wife and I were advised to keep our car doors securely locked when travelling on the city streets. We were warned never to roll down our windows to display our generosity to street children who flocked to the traffic intersections, much like here in Delhi. This would, we were assured, be the surest way to risking life and limb or both to dangerous marauders who fronted as innocent children, or worse, created the opportunity for loot by more lethal highwaymen lurking in the shadows. Not a very happy setting for cross-cultural engagement you would think. At one of our first forays on to the mean streets, we stopped at a traffic signal at a major intersection and had a swarm of animated children tapping at our car windows, insistent that we reward them for their impromptu acrobatics or off-key musical renditions. We kept looking straight ahead, ignoring the commotion outside, praying that this threatening apparition would soon pass with a change in the traffic signal. But having tried every trick in the trade, the boys soon came up with an ace up their sleeve. They burst into a passable rendering of the then popular Hindi film song, *Kuch Kuch Hota Hai*, but with an enthusiasm which melted all resistance and led, inexorably, to the rolling down of the glass barrier that separated us. That was our first lesson in the Indonesian version of cross-cultural conversation, courtesy a bunch of street kids, and we never looked back thereafter.

I wish to speak of another experience in nearby Kathmandu. I had invited the well-known vocalist Pandit Jasraj to sing before an audience that was allowed to invite itself by picking up invitation cards from different locations in the city on a first come first served basis. We were delighted to see that the overwhelming majority of the large audience were in fact young Nepalis from the Kathmandu Valley. After the predictably magical performance, we were in for another surprise. A long line of youngsters had formed spontaneously to greet the great maestro and seek his blessings, touching his feet in a traditional gesture of deep respect. At that moment I felt profoundly humbled. Here was an individual who had effortlessly achieved in a single evening what I could never hope to accomplish in a lifetime of official diplomacy. I felt sad that India so underutilized one of its most powerful assets in the conduct of its diplomacy.

Mere tolerance for ways of life or patterns of thinking different from our own is not sufficient basis for cross-cultural engagement. It is, rather, the willingness to understand and to appreciate what lies behind those differences. The exploration of another culture is like reading a book in which each page you turn holds the key to another hundred. Not everyone has the opportunity or the time and patience to do this. Those who do, owe it others to interpret for and guide others on their journeys, dispelling prejudice and fostering understanding. It seems to me, as a layman not as a theorist, that some cultures like ours are aural, where sound and the spoken word are the preferred medium of communication. Others like the Chinese are visual cultures, where the symbolic image and the written character are its defining features.

The most ancient treaties in Sanskrit like the Vedas, the Puranas and the Upanishads are classified as 'Smritis', or what has been remembered and committed to memory, or 'Shrutis', or what has been heard and recorded from the ancient sages. The correct pronunciation of the various mantras is particularly important. The power of an invocation derives from the subtle vibrations that its chanting creates.

For an Indian learning Chinese characters, which I had to, as a student, it was difficult but at the same time a fascinating and rare opportunity to slowly lay bare the inner sanctums of a civilization more ancient and perhaps more complex than our own. Consider some of the Chinese characters.

The earliest Chinese characters were pictographs, close to the objects they represented. Let us see how some of the most basic characters evolved, over a period of 5,000 years.

Figure 6.1: Evolution of Chinese Ideograms over the Past 5,000 Years

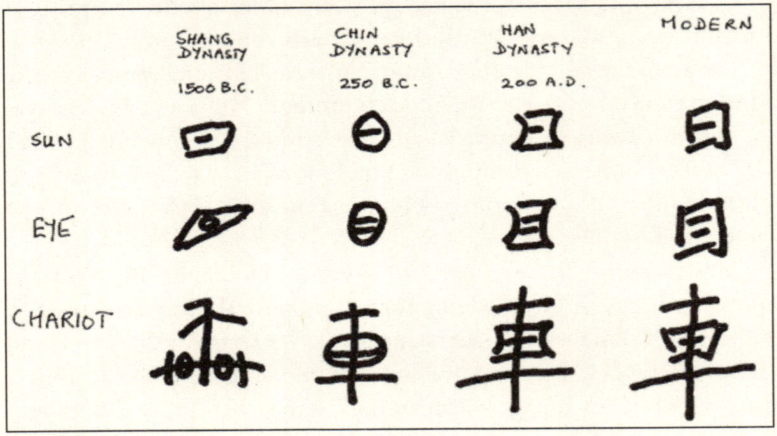

Source: Author.

Then there are pictorials that later evolved into more generic concepts. For example, the symbol for well-being and the word good is a woman with a child. The word peace is represented by a woman with a roof over her head. A family is symbolized by a sow with several piglets feeding at her udders and they too have a roof to shelter them against the elements. All these symbols are in one sense strange, but at the same time incredibly universal in the concepts they portray.

And then there is the concept of time. In Chinese, the word for day before yesterday is, literally, 'front day', while the day after tomorrow

Figure 6.2: Conceptual Characters

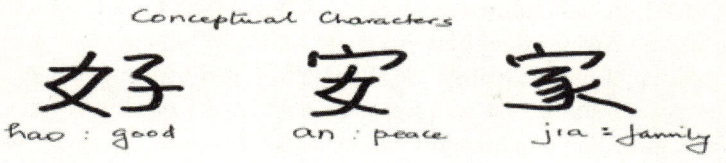

Conceptual Characters

好 hao : good　　安 an : peace　　家 jia = family .

Source: Author.

is represented by the symbols 'back-day' or the day to the rear. I would always confuse the two and my teacher would get extremely frustrated. I explained to her that in most parts of the world, people thought of the past as being behind one's back, while the future always lies in the front. What I was being asked to accept, I said, with an air of superior logic, was to reverse this natural ordering. My teacher looked at me with some pity and explained patiently: the past is something we have already experienced, it is no longer a closed book, therefore it is in front of us. The future we have not yet seen and hence it lies behind us. Could I dispute this? I could not. And thus was born a healthy respect for a viewpoint different from one's own.

The test for a diplomat often comes when he is dealing with an adversarial situation where it is required to convey an unpleasant message to his interlocutor, unambiguously and firmly and yet remain within the bounds of courtesy and politeness. A diplomat will never exacerbate an already unpleasant situation. His job is to keep temperatures cool even as he seeks to uphold his country's position. A diplomat who plays to the gallery is in the wrong profession. To convey a tough message when required but without raising one's voice, to resist the temptation to answer provocative behaviour with even greater stridency, these are cultivated skills which hopefully become innate over time. And this is where a broader backdrop of cross-cultural understanding, the ability to put the present and the current in a civilizational context, is fundamental to the craft of diplomacy.

We live in a world today where there are two competing and often clashing forces at work. At one end of the spectrum, the transport and communication revolution has brought humanity much closer than at any time in history. There are vastly greater opportunities to directly experience other cultures or learn about them through virtual media. There is continual exposure to different ways of life, cultural norms and traditions and cuisine. This is leading to the enrichment of different cultures, a growing appreciation of the best which every country and culture has to offer and making us more aware of the cultural particularities of our extended neighbourhood. This is the basis on which we develop a sensitivity about and respect for deeply held beliefs and convictions of people different from us. The intensity of this interaction is leading to a burst of creativity and intellectual ferment across the world and this is welcome. However, there is another darker force that has been unleashed by the very same proximity, leading to fears about a loss of identity, a sense of being culturally adrift in a world being transformed with unprecedented rapidity. This retards the process of engagement and dialogue not only between cultures but within cultures and between generations. Instead of celebrating diversity and sharing, we begin to raise walls around us and seek to stifle the very influences that keep our own culture alive and vibrant. A culture that does not share will soon stagnate and die.

I believe that open and liberal societies, in particular plural democracies like ours, are far better equipped to deal with the increasingly congested world that is emerging, where the ability to deal with diversity and adapt to different cultures will be the hallmark of a great and successful power. India is a classic crossroads culture, shaped in history by the maritime exchange that its peninsular character made possible both with the eastern as well as western reaches of the Indian Ocean. It is also comfortable with the caravan culture of Central Asia, having influenced and itself in turn been influenced by the constant infusion of goods, peoples and ideas across centuries. It is in our genes to be comfortable with a globalized and interconnected world. We have been there before, though the present scale of interaction and the pace of change is admittedly frenetic.

In rising to our destiny, we need to be careful that we do not devalue the very strengths we possess as a confident and accommodative culture. We must not encourage a political culture which feeds on division, exploiting fears of the loss of identity and creating a sense of siege. We must reject the intolerance we see towards the expression of views or portrayal in art which diverge from narrowly defined cultural categories or uninformed prejudices. If we are to engage other cultures in a productive dialogue, we must reaffirm confidence in our own and learn to accept and celebrate the diversity that lies at the heart of our democracy.

There is another trend that I worry about. The global war on terrorism has spawned a pervasive environment of fear and suspicion which exacerbates the intolerance and prejudice I referred to. Proud and liberal democracies, including our own, have become increasingly complicit in the surrender of precious freedoms in the mistaken belief that this is unavoidable in the interest of keeping us safe from terrorism. Everyone becomes a suspect. An encounter with a stranger is no longer pregnant with the possibility of a new and exciting experience, a valued friendship or a window to a world differently perceived. He could, we fear, be a source of elemental danger. Little by little, slice after slice, our privacy is invaded, our words and actions are monitored, our conversations are tapped and analyzed by those who thrive on promoting fear. Very soon we shall have virtually every aspect of our lives peeled open, layer upon layer like an onion. This feeds the coercive power of the state and its innately predatory instincts. We are becoming societies where security agencies increasingly exercise a veto over the choices of elected governments. This is justified by the state and increasingly rationalized and acquiesced into by its citizens as the price we must pay to be safe in a post-Osama Bin Laden world. This slide towards authoritarianism is becoming insidiously internalized.

One sees with rising alarm as the most powerful bastion of liberal democracy, individual freedom and constitutionally guaranteed freedom of expression, the United States, brings its technological genius to unleash a cumulative process of abridging the very values that have attracted millions to its shores and sustained its intellectual creativity. How quickly has it put in place a most comprehensive and efficient machine to invade the innermost secrets of its own citizens and those who are not violating their privacy and even their person, all in the name of keeping the homeland secure. And I see the danger that we in India will follow suit. We hear expressions of admiration of how America has successfully prevented terrorist acts by putting in place this surveillance machine and our agencies are eager to learn from its example.

I see another threat to our plural and liberal democratic traditions and this time in the association of high growth rate and economic success with political authoritarianism. China's success is admirable but it is not our way and should never be. The seemingly unbeatable blend of market economics and totalitarian politics is not the wave of the future, certainly not India's future.

In an article that appeared just a couple of days ago, entitled "2011: A Brave New Dystopia",[1] by Chris Hedges, who wrote the book *Death of the Liberal Class*, takes us back to two very prescient works, George Orwell's *1984* and Aldous Huxley's *Brave New World*. "Orwell", he says "warned of a world where books were banned. Huxley warned of a world where no one wanted to read books". And again, "Orwell saw us frightened into submission. Huxley saw us seduced into submission". We see these warning signs all around us.

The danger is that unless an informed and enlightened citizenry resists such tendencies, the lines between the politics of authoritarianism that we decry in totalitarian states and that which is creeping upon our own free and open societies may become increasingly blurred. "Big Brother is Watching You" used to be the hallmark of totalitarian societies. It must never become the defining feature of democratic societies. This is not an environment in which cross-cultural communication, which we celebrate at this conference, will be able to survive, let alone thrive. Societies pervaded by fear will fear everything, including talking to a friend, let alone a stranger. The Chinese writer and activist, Liu Xiaobo who won the Nobel Peace Prize this year, warned against this destructive fear which breeds repression. One desperately needs a Liu Xiaobo in our own free societies, too, to declare, loud and clear, on our behalf, "I have no enemies".

NOTE AND REFERENCE

1. Chris Hedges, Senior Fellow at the Nation Institute, 'Brave New Dystopia'. Available online at www.truthdig.com (accessed 27 December 2010).

7

Politics of Democracy and the Politics of Religion in a Post-secular Age[1]

Ashis Nandy

I

I cannot now remember when exactly I lost and, then, was forced to rediscover religion. But I know that the loss was due to the sudden expansion of my world brought about by my encounter with the terribly sceptical, intellectual culture of mid-twentieth century Calcutta. I was then in my teens. Perhaps the spirit of youthful rebellion against authorities had something to do with it; my parents were devout believers like many of their generation. My friends and our younger teachers were often non-believers, though probably not as aggressively as they pretended. I rediscovered religion after about 35 years, very slowly and very reluctantly. The change was not precipitated by any personal crisis, new-found spiritual sentiments or faith, but by a concern with the fate of democracies globally, especially in the South. I had also over the years become aware of the massive violence unleashed by the secular states on their own innocent citizens. Some of the worst records of genocide were held by secular states. The rediscovery was to acquire other emotional and political associations, too, but they are not that relevant to our concerns here.

For reasons I have not yet fully grasped, the political geography of both religion and democracy began to change after World War II and the changes began to become more apparent during the 1970s and 1980s. I myself was an interested spectator and a product of those times. First, suddenly the number of democracies in the world grew from about a dozen to more than 100 and the world population living under democracy quadrupled. Most of these were newly independent countries, freed from colonialism, and it soon became obvious tha in many of these new democracies, sizeable sections of the citizens were exercising their democratic rights not to push their individual claims, but to push their collective cultural, religious or communal demands. Such demands were always there in democracies but in the older democracies, on the one hand, the demands had become more predictable and manageable. When not so, they were usually the demands of small noisy minorities, often easily dismissed as a lunatic fringe or as harmless eccentrics. In the new democracies on the other hand, these demands looked strange, dangerous, unpredictable and primordial even to the modern leadership, media and sections of the middle class within the countries. The borderlines among culture, religion and community looked blurred. Such demands naturally aroused widespread anxiety and fear in the older democracies and among the first-generation ruling elite in Asia and Africa.

Second, and simultaneously, there grew the fear of what the newly enfranchised citizens in the new democracies were bringing into politics by way of cultural preferences. These included new styles and values in governance, indeed new protocols of democracy. These protocols often encompassed new styles of nepotism and corruption, new forms of reverence and irreverence and new hierarchies of ideological and non-ideological commitments. In these, too, there was the tacit presence of religion. In the sense that political actors often seemed terribly under-socialized in existing patterns of expectation from democratic politics, the law-and-order machinery and a secular state. In some cases they lifted public values and cognitive frames straight from their diverse religious worldviews.

Third, democracy may or may not succeed in distributing economic and social power, but it always redistributes charisma. Indeed, democracy can be redefined as an institutionalized means of decentralizing and redistributing charisma. In a democracy, however imperfect, charisma tends to be unstable and labile; frequently it refuses to remain concentrated in designated persons or institutions; it has a long-term, secular tendency to get redistributed among ordinary citizens. Terms like 'masses', 'people', 'taxpayers' and even 'citizens' have come to share the charisma that was once the virtual monopoly of royalties and aristocracies.[2]

Even when charisma looks heavily concentrated in non-traditional domains, such as cinema and sports, it is transient and decentralized. There is no sophisticated attempt to legitimize it, no grand social or political theory and certainly no theology. In the domain of religions too, in parts of the world, while the importance of charismatic religious leaders and evangelists have grown, the Church, the Ulema or the clergy no longer looks that awe-inspiring and exclusive. Old-style evangelism may be flourishing, but new forms of self-induced conversion or choosing another religion in addition to one's own, without actually converting, is also becoming more common. This expansion of religious choice—it includes also smaller choices that cut across religious lines, such as the growing popularity of yoga, Tibetan healing traditions and Christian marriage rituals among non-Christian communities—have made many religious leaders and defenders of faith nervous and doubly defensive. They suspect they are living in a new, uncertain, strange world and they try to cope with their fears through cognitive closure. The same fears and the same closure can be seen among those allegiant to the new religion-substitutes of our times, nationalism and secularism. In Turkey, France and India, for instance, any interrogation of such faiths are seen as virtually unnatural acts.

Fourth, it has become obvious that in the South the encounter with aggressively evangelical Christianity during the colonial times has produced among some of the major faiths a reaction that psychoanalysts will call 'identification with the aggressor'—an attempt to produce from within their ranks revised—read revised or edited—versions of faith that can stand up to the evangelical challenge of masculine, Protestant Christianity by being its mirror image. These attempts are fired by the conviction that such reworked versions of religion are more compatible with modernity, national state and industrial capitalism. In South Asia, for instance, both Hinduism and Buddhism, though considered ancient faiths, have produced their own versions of Protestant reform movements such as Brahmo Samaj (founded 1830), Arya Samaj (1875), Ramakrishna Mission (1897) and Mahabodhi Society (1891) and reformers such as Ram Mohan Roy (1772–1822), Dayananda Saraswati (1824–1883),

Swami Vivekananda (1863–1920) and Anagarika Dharmapala (1864–1933). Only small groups of people actually opted for belief systems these movements propagated, but they changed the entire culture of religion. To this extent, Hinduism and Buddhism as we know them today in urban, middle-class South Asia are all new faiths, not much more than a century old. (For the moment, I am not discussing the case of South Asian Islam because similar movements in Islam acquired momentum later and their influence became obvious even later. One should be able to say Islam, too, is becoming a new faith today.)

The most important, the common core, of these projects has been a two-fold attempt to brush up their faiths. The overt part of the effort is to make them more compatible with modern rationality and scientific spirit and cleanse them of 'superstitions', 'meaningless' rituals and local customs that have come to be associated with them. This has been accompanied by determined attempts to give theology—including its 'philosophical' basis—absolute priority over rituals, rites and practices. The more covert goals has been to use these means to centralize the faiths, give them well-marked borders and make them more compatible, manageable and subservient to the demands of a modern nation state and its ideas of secularism and the needs of a modern, urban-industrial society.

Responding to these processes and occasionally rebelling against them, there have been efforts to reimagine the relationship and open a more self-confident, open-ended dialogue between politics and religion during the last four decades. We all know of such initiatives and all I have to do here is to mention, as examples, three of them that have been prominent.

First, religion has re-emerged as an epic of the oppressed and as a language of resistance. Some of the African American churches that emerged out of the experience of slavery, post-World War II liberation theology in Christianity and Ali Shariati in Islam are examples. I say re-emerged, not emerged, because this is a use of religion known to all religions since ancient times. It has been rediscovered because the fond nineteenth century belief that this-worldly, science-based, secular knowledge will supply theories of liberation more appropriate for our times lies shattered and discredited all around us. At the same time, with the decline of the secular power of organized religion, the priestly classes no longer look so formidable, despite the return and spread of fundamentalism in many parts of the world.

Second, the spreading belief that the processes of disenchantment and desacralization have gone too far has led to determined efforts to reclaim some areas of life from, what look like, clutches of the secular, for purposes of resacralization. Some of the most conspicuous of these areas are environment, reproductivity (as an antipode or negation of productivity), childhood and life itself.

Third, the major South Asian faiths do not have centralized, overarching, church-like structures that can be engaged, appeased or bargained with. This has led to the emergence of new kinds of political formations that try to act like brokers between the state and highly diverse religious communities but have no intrinsic sanction in the community to do so. However, they do enjoy political support among some sections of the urban, educated, modernized or semi-modernized middle classes that have moved towards an idea of religion as a standardized, generic, global belief system. These formations can thus also act as political pressure groups in a democratic order and begin to influence public policy under certain circumstances.

There are other important processes at work too. But the ones I have mentioned have most influenced my work on religion and politics, particularly my critique of secularism and my fascination with Mohandas Gandhi's maxim that it is impossible to imagine politics without religion. The rest of this chapter is a brief introduction to my position on the subject. It is heavily indebted to a serial trialogue among Michio Araki, Charles Long and me that Araki organized. That intellectual exchange has remained a memorable and formative influence me.

II

No one thought that religion would re-emerge from the shadows to occupy centre stage at the beginning of the twenty-first century. Many wrote obituaries of religions as early as in the middle of the nineteenth century. Since then, it has been the triumph of one secular ideology after another, though steep decline or ignominious fall has usually followed the triumph. Religion has re-emerged at the end of what could be called an age of ideologies, not in its pristine form but bearing the imprint and, sometimes, even the garb of the age of secular ideologies. At the beginning of the twenty-first century, religion is a phoenix that has risen from its own ashes and wears the ashes as a sign of its new triumph.

This may or may not be an enigma. The attempts to banish all mystery and spirituality from life, the increasing poverty of the individualism that envelops lonely crowds in fully developed consuming societies, the steady growth of violence, often gratuitous, the decline in the sanctity of life that finds expression not only in wars, machine violence and torture but also in assaults on the environment and the life-support system of the coming generations, widespread use of the Enlightenment values as justifications for new forms of dominance and despotism—they all have eroded the easy faith in the age of reason and the boundless power of human reason.[3]

At the same time, the religious worldview is a worldview after all and, like all worldviews, it too carries a baggage. After the crusades and the holy wars, the genocide of indigenous peoples in the Americas, slavery and colonialism sanctioned by powerful sections of the Christian church and the more recent rise in religion-based terrorism in the Islamic world and the blatant secular use of religion in South Asian politics—where Hinduism, Islam, Buddhism and Sikhism have been periodically used to mobilize hatred—we cannot but admit that the domain of religion parallels the domain of secular politics and can harbour as much gratuitous violence, paranoia and sadomasochism. It is true that one look at R.J. Rummell's data and some rough arithmetical manipulation of them reveal that in the last hundred years fully secular states have killed at least 45 times as many people as religious violence and fundamentalism have done.[4] But then, as Charles Long likes to say, "secularism is a hidden religion for which no one has to take any responsibility". It is safer to presume that, given opportunities, people will kill, rape and plunder in the name of religion as happily as people have done in the name of secular statecraft, nationalism, progress, revolution and development.

Only two things have changed. First, whatever may have happened in the past, the violence that religion now sanctions cannot compete in range and depth with the violence that modern states sanction in the name of secular ideologies. Second, being primarily interest-based and a pathology of rationality, state violence has increasingly become more organized, scientific, efficient and user-friendly, whereas religion violence, to the extent it is passion-based and a pathology of irrationality, leaves loopholes and spaces for inefficiency and, hence, offers more scope for individual and collective resistance. I hasten to add, though, that these differences are getting smudged; in its new incarnation, religious violence too is acquiring many of the features of state violence.

Why should then we negotiate the domain of religion as citizens? Why should we learn the language of religion or enter the cosmology of religion? The honest answer is that we do not have to, except as ethnographers, historians or psychologists. At one time it must have been different, but now millions of people live without the benefit of faith. It is unlikely that one would run out of company if one refuses to learn the language or enter the cosmology of religion. One can easily converse with a sizeable number of people in the academe, in professions and in the higher echelons of the state who speak the language of secular statecraft and individual citizenship.

However, an even larger part of the world and a huge majority of those staying in the godforsaken parts of the world—in Latin America, Africa and Asia—have partial or no access to the language of secularism and citizenship. Often they have been denied such citizenship, though invited to use the language of citizenship. Anyone who refuses to learn the language and the cosmology of religion has, as a result, little or no access to that other world. This is no great loss if you are a modern academic in a modern university, or if you plan to live exclusively within the confines of one of the many pockets of modernity that pockmark the southern hemisphere. I am fully aware that mostly the poor, the marginal, the retrogressive and the disposable today seem to have religion. However, if you happen to be one of those who take democratic participation seriously or seek to influence public life and public policy in the southern world, it becomes a different story.

This is because, without some access to the religious worldview, you will pretty soon become primarily a spectator of politics and left with only two options: constantly bemoaning the bad choices that 'ignorant', 'ill-informed', 'irrational' electorates make and shedding copious tears on the rise of religious fundamentalism and ethnic chauvinism under competitive democracy. You will also have to, I am afraid, reconcile yourself to lamenting the way the ungodly and the ill-motivated occupy increasingly larger public space just because they speak the language of religion and can converse from within a religious worldview. If you are enterprising enough, you might console yourself by writing angry columns in newspapers or letters to editors or talk of the good old days when politics and politicians were reportedly purer and more idealistic.

This is not a convoluted plea to return to faith or to establish the superiority of the language of religion. It is a plea to acknowledge the costs of democracy. In a democracy, citizens have the right to bring their ethical frameworks within politics and these frameworks may not please their well wishers ever-ready to speak on behalf of the people. No sloganeering on the need to keep separate religion and politics—the church and the state—can work on those whose everyday ethics are directly or indirectly derived from religion, especially since we cannot employ a thought police to force citizens to maintain such separation.[5] It is a pity, I am sure, that despite more than three hundred years of spirited, dedicated efforts, so many still use religious cosmology as a ballast in life, particularly when buffeted by the disorienting pace of social change, uprooting or personal insecurity. Many of us may not need such a ballast, but we cannot ensure that in a democracy others would not. The situation has been complicated in recent decades by the growing trend in many secular, modern states to set up as a political ploy entire religions and civilizations as demonic others that need to be defanged. Those at the receiving end of such stereotype are naturally finding it increasingly difficult to adore the secular worldview as intrinsically opposed to fanaticism and hatred.[6]

Here the African Americans in the United States have a lesson to offer to Africa and Asia, particularly to the South Asian intellectuals tirelessly speaking of the virtues of secularism. No one can deny that Christianity was virtually imposed on the community. But by now, their Christianity bears the mark of their suffering over two centuries. They have made something out of that imposition that is distinctively theirs. Christianity in turn, I dare say, has been at its creative best when deployed as a theology of emancipation by the African Americans and African Africans. From Reverend Martin Luther King to Reverend Desmond Tutu, it has been the unfolding of the potentialities of an Asian faith that defy the European heritage of Christianity to supply a potent political philosophy of militant non-violence that has radically changed our ideas of political resistance and dissent. (This Christianity, conversing with the Hindu–Jain traditions through Gandhi, has also initiated a remarkable dialogue of faiths in our times outside the academe.) It has sought to emancipate European Christianity from some of its conventionalities and its historical baggage, the baggage that prompted Mohandas Gandhi to say that Christianity was a good religion before it went to Europe. I need hardly add that the Truth and Reconciliation Commission in South Africa was not a secular enterprise. Nor was it a sui generis brainwave of Tutu. It was squarely located in an ecumenical frame that cut across faiths and ideologies, beliefs and disbeliefs. In the commission, religion entered politics in a way that Gandhi would have applauded. Like others, I know the deficiencies of the commission, but they do not detract from the daring ethical imagination that inspired the project.[7]

There is another lesson for us in the African American experience. Through all their struggles, they never yielded ground to the religious fanatics though there were small, identifiable groups within them pushing towards extremism. Because the community's leadership never abandoned the sphere of religion as irrelevant to the public life, some of the most creative inputs into their struggle for equality and dignity came from within their religious consciousness. Those who opposed fanaticism and bigotry among them could make sense to others in their community because they shared the language of religion. I could give similar examples from Latin America, the Sandinistas being one of the most conspicuous among them. The Sandinista cabinet included a number of priests and was headed by one, and the movement they represented, whatever its other flaws, never lost touch with the religious self of their constituency. It is not true that all shades of Marxism have to embrace, with fundamentalist fervour, the secularist dogma.

In India, in contrast, the first generation of post-independence leaders were reverent but fearful of Gandhi and his 'intemperate' use of religion in politics. Some of them, to the delight 'progressives', quickly shifted to a political idiom that was an insipid copy of social-democratic ideologies floating around in Europe, especially Fabian socialism of the inter-war years, leavened with a pinch of the hard materialism of the Leninist kind.

They declared the entire domain of religion untouchable and left it to its 'natural' carriers—the 'backward', 'illiterate', 'provincial' apprentice-citizens of the society.[8]

The results of that short-sightedness and obeisance to transient fashions had to be disastrous, when tinged with tacit fear and contempt for a mostly rural, obstinately traditional citizens in an Asian society. Taking advantage of this, small groups of Hindu, Muslim, Buddhist and Sikh political activists have begun to arbitrarily claim the right to speak on behalf of these religions. These claims have not been seriously challenged, for the credibility of those speaking on religious matters from within modernity is low.

The modern intelligentsia in India, lacking the ability to assess matters of religion, have also mechanically accepted the credentials of the small-time political activists speaking for entire religious communities, whether such activists are psychopathic, violence-prone, rabble-rousers trying to break into politics or scheming, paranoiac, necrophilic political leaders. One of the saddest spectacles in India in recent years has been the effort of some Catholic religious figures to open a dialogue with the unelected, self-proclaimed leaders of Hindus like the Rashtriya Swayam Sevak Sangh (RSS) and the Vishwa Hindu Parishad (VHP). These are formations that claim to speak for all Hindus of the world—the one billion of them—when they and the parties they support have together never won even one-third of Hindu votes in India.

★★★

There is a built-in contradiction in my argument here. I have made a case for understanding religious worldviews as means of entering popular consciousness and the normative frames that shape India democracy and its future. Yet, it remains an open question how far these worldviews by themselves shape the democratic culture and how far their influence is processed through the packaged positions on religion floating around in the public sphere.[9]

Fortunately, do not feel obliged to believe in a manner acceptable to philosophers, theologians and historians of religion. Nor do they fully trust the politicians when it comes to religion. For most believers, religion is a matter of periodic participation in rituals and other modest observances. When they speak of religion, they have in mind simple, everyday versions of faith that look anti-philosophical and are often an embarrassment to sophisticated believers. Perhaps in these humble practices there are some built-in respect for—and celebration of—a sacralized cosmos and sanctity of life that allows highly diverse visions of a desirable society to flourish.

As I have grown old, in my work on religion I have increasingly underplayed the canonical texts and practices (the so-called high culture of religion) to emphasize the lowbrow and the non-canonical, contaminated by ordinary people and everyday life. One reason for this is that the modern state has always felt more comfortable with the high culture of religion and shown a preference for the centralized and the well organized as opposed to the decentralized and the ill-organized.[10]

In South Asia, what was left undone by the colonial administrators, perpetually looking for a single, definitive version of the faiths—so that the colonial states could cope with, manage or arrive at a political quid pro quo with native religions—was completed by the modern university system, ever eager to identify the 'real' form and core of a religion. As a result today, Arab Islam has become the main tradition of Islam only, redefining the world's larger Islamic societies as abodes of peripheral Islam; Manusamhita has become the final, authoritative text on Hindu law, thanks to the efforts of the colonial dispensation to codify Hindu law; and Anagarika Dhammapala's ethno-nationalist Buddhism has trumped the older traditions of Buddhism in Sri Lanka.

These redefinitions have been gradually internalized by large sections of modern, educated believers in the Asia and Africa. We are paying for this now. The pathetic effort of many Muslim communities to defend their religious identity and self-esteem, by opting for a blood-drenched version of 'pure' Islam, is only one part of the story. For one sees a similar development in a number of other religions, in which the axis of self-definition has shifted under the onslaught of a new, 'universal' idea of faith popularized by the nineteenth century European universities and knowledge systems.

Second, the religious worldview, being a worldview, always has within it a place for irreverence, wit and play. The global triumph of European Protestantism during the nineteenth and twentieth centuries, especially its close links with industrial capitalism and colonialism, and its ability to underwrite a housebroken version of religion that is subservient to the nation state, have strengthened some forms of Puritanism in virtually every major religion. Some of the non-Semitic, 'pagan' creeds have been particularly unfortunate in this regard. A large majority of their followers are accustomed to some degree of playfulness, show of irreverence, familiarity and bargaining with gods and goddesses, eroticism and ethical latitude even in the domain of the sacred. Th s has begun to embarrass many believers exposed to Calvinist cultures of religion, who feel even more offended if someone from outside the fold is audacious enough to presume the same intimacy with the gods and goddesses, thereby drawing attention to the 'pagan' elements of their faiths. What was a source of strength in these faiths has, thus, become an excuse for censorship and xenophobia.

One final comment before I end. We are probably entering a period when the decisive battle will be not between fundamentalism and secularism or between identity politics and normal, interest-based politics. The battle may well be between religion in its new, packaged, consumer-friendly version as a political ideological platform and the subversive spiritualities—to steal Frederique Apffel Marglin's evocative expression—that are breaking out at the peripheries and the underside our known world.

NOTES AND REFERENCES

1. The second part of the chapter has undergone many incarnations. It began as a public conversation among Michio Araki, Charles Long and me. The present version specifically draws upon the C.R. Parekh Lecture, 'Return of the Sacred: Politics of Religion in a Post-Secular Age', 2008, delivered at the University of Westminster, London, and the Mahesh Chandra Regmi Lecture given at Kathmandu on 13 December 2007.

2. This redistribution affects everyone living in a democracy. The way President John F. Kennedy's sexual escapades were treated by the media and the American public was not the way President Bill Clinton's were treated. Likewise, discretion with which President Mitterrand's illegitimate daughter was allowed to become public knowledge towards the end of his life has not been evident in the case of President Nicolas Sarkozy's sexual life. The charisma attaching to presidency, it can be argued, is differently and perhaps more thinly concentrated in the presidency in both countries now.

3. See for instance Alister McGrath, *The Twilight of Atheism: The Rise and Fall of Disbelief in the Modern World* (New York: Doubleday, 2004). An instance of the growing doubts

about the efficacy of secularism within political theory is William E. Connolly, *Why I am not a Secularist* (Minneapolis: University of Minnesota, 1999).
4. R.J. Rummel, *Death by Government: Genocide and Mass Murder Since 1900* (West Hanover, Mass.: Christopher Publishing, 1994).
5. For that matter, there is little evidence in contemporary psychology that people can maintain such separation within themselves on a long-term basis. Indeed, there is much evidence that they try to reduce such dissonance. While there is some evidence that South Asians can live with greater cognitive dissonance within themselves, this capacity is in decline in the urban melting pots of the region, where most religious violence takes place.
6. On this subject, see, for instance, Asma Barlas, 'The Secular Commitment to "Islamic Fundamentalism"', *Daily Times,* 4 August 2002. Barlas says at one place,

> ... one could argue, for instance, that whereas in the West, modernity brought the benefits of capitalism, industrialization, and representative democracy, for most of the world, it brought colonization, slavery, economic ruin, a militarization of politics, increased poverty, the extinction of indigenous people and cultural alienation. Similarly, the very secularism that freed 'man'—in the masculinist language of the Enlightenment—from the alleged tyranny of religion, also opened up to doubt people's sense of themselves as purposive moral agents in the world. Hence, what some embraced as freedom, others experienced as profound loss.

For a powerful, detailed treatment of the issue, see Ali Mazrui, '"Progress": Illegitimate Child of Judeo-Christian Universalism and Western Ethnocentrism—A Third World Critique', in Bruce Mazlish and Leo Marx (eds), *Progress: Fact or Illusion* (Ann Arbor: University of Michigan, 1996), 153–74. Strangely, such arguments, when made in the context of Islam, are more acceptable in academic circles in India than when made in the context of Hinduism.
7. For a glimpse into Tutu's own way of looking at the commission, see Desmond Tutu, *No Future without Forgiveness* (London: Rider, 1999).
8. The discomfort with religion in public life in a society organized around religion and the culture of avoidance and denial the discomfort produces is illustrated by the absence of a single department of religious studies in any of India's roughly 350 universities, even though many of them are modelled on famous western universities known for their departments of religious studies.
9. Elsewhere I have argued that most of these packaged software come not as religious cults or sects but as religion-based political ideologies that do not include any theory of transcendence. See for instance, Ashis Nandy, 'The Politics of Secularism and the Recovery of Religious Tolerance', in Ashis Nandy (ed.), *Time Warps: The Insistent Politics of Silent and Evasive Pasts* (New Delhi: Permanent Black, 2001), 61–88; and Ashis Nandy, 'The Twilight of Certitudes: Secularism, Hindu Nationalism and Other Masks of Deculturation', in Ashis Nandy (ed.), *The Romance of the State and the Fate Dissent in the Tropics* (New Delhi: Oxford University Press, 2003), 61–82.
10. Interested readers may like to look up Ashis Nandy, 'A Report on the Present State of Health of Gods and Goddesses in India', in Ashis Nandy (ed.), *Time Warps: The Insistent Politics of Silent and Evasive Pasts* (New Delhi: Permanent Black, 2002), 129–56; and 'The Twilight of Certitudes'.

8

Bridging Divide: The Triumph of Bollywood

Madhu Purnima Kishwar

Obsession with the outside world's perception of us is typically confined to educated elite groups in our country. In the mental landscapes of poor farmers, impoverished weavers, exploited and harassed cycle rickshaw pullers or garbage pickers in our cities, there is hardly any space for personal or national vanities. Far more important to them is whether their lives' trials and tribulations are of concern to those in power or those who influence the wielders of power.

In sharp contrast, the elite sections of Indian society, especially those who are privileged enough to travel to opulent First World nations or are living and working there, are hypersensitive about how the world views India, because that perception determines how they are treated when they go abroad.

Till the advent of half-hearted economic reforms in India in the early 1990s, the predominant image of India was that of an 'underdeveloped third world country'. Deep down, Indians too had imbibed this view of themselves and their society. Most people had come to believe that India's stagnant economy did not allow talent to flourish. Therefore the most ambitious among them did all they could to escape their motherland by migrating to First World countries of the West. Procuring a US green card or citizenship were the acme of ambition for the aspiring classes of India. The outmigration of India's educated elite was justified on the ground that 'brain drain is better than brain in the drain'.

On the economic front, a modest dose of liberalization in the last two decades has brought about a dramatic change in the perception of India and the self-view of the Indian elite classes. The Indian corporate sector has emerged globally triumphant and instead of being swamped by Western MNCs, Indian corporates are not only floating their own MNCs but also taking over well-established American and European MNCs, despite racial prejudice and negative stereotyping of Indians. For example, when India's steel magnate Lakshmi Narayan Mittal wanted to acquire Arcelor, his offer was originally mocked as 'monkey money from an Indian'. Arcelor directors put so many hurdles in his path that in the end Mittal ended up paying a much higher price for the acquisition which was described by many interested business watchers as 'the Hindu premium', or a special levy for his coming from a supposedly backward and oppressive culture.

But when the steel magnate turned the fortunes of the company and emerged as the third richest man in the world, as the only global steel producer in the world with operations in 14 countries, spanning over four continents, the Western corporate world looked at his spreading empire with awe and reverence. So fast have the image of India Inc. changed that after acquiring iconic automobile company Jaguar, Ratan Tata thought nothing of publicly chastising the British managers for their lax work ethic, saying they are only worried about their next weekend and are 'not willing to go the extra mile unlike their Indian counterparts'.

Today, the image of India in the business schools of the West is that of a burgeoning economy with an entrepreneurial class capable of competing with the best. Bangalore, Hyderabad, Chennai and Gurgaon, as throbbing hubs of information technology, have become the new icons of India. At least 30 per cent of the start-up enterprises in Silicon Valley are started or backed by Indians.

US VERSUS THEM

One of the outstanding achievements of our freedom movement under the leadership of Gandhi was that people of different strata, castes, communities, regions and economic sectors were brought together to form an effective coalition on the common platform provided by the refurbished Congress Party. This allowed them to articulate their specific grievances and get a measure of support from each other. Gandhi tried to create an atmosphere whereby a significant section of the wealthy and the relatively powerful groups began to use their clout not just for their own narrow self-interest but also to help those belonging to marginalized groups. The collective energy thus generated was directed at bringing about political freedom for India without needless violence and other destructive modes of expressing people's political aspirations that have been common in many other freedom movements across the globe.

The increasing emotional gap between the urban elite and the rural population is even more glaring. The urban elite often use the word *dehat'* (literal meaning 'one who resides in a village') to derisively refer to someone who is ignorant, stupid and uncouth. This 'us' and 'they' divide and the mindset to treat the basic survival needs of the poor with callous disregard is reflected in every aspect of our national life. City planners forget to allocate space for street vendors in their eagerness to provide fashionable malls, even though street vendors are no less, if not more vital to the health of our city economy. Our planners leave no space on the city roads and on our national highways for non-motorized vehicles while spending all their energies on making high speed motorways and flyovers even though tens of crores of people have to use these slow-moving vehicles for commuting as well as carrying goods. The elite are busy building islands of opulence and prosperity for themselves amidst poverty and squalor, living in gated communities.

With 1.2 billion people, India is the largest democracy in the world, a laboratory among developing countries for testing how well democracy is able to accommodate and improve the lives of a huge population. India is richer than ever before, with rising global influence. Yet its development is divisive at home. It is experiencing a Gilded Age of nouveau billionaires while it is cleaved by inequality and plagued in some states by poverty and malnutrition levels rivalling sub-Saharan Africa.

ASPIRATIONS OF INDIA INC. VESUS REST OF INDIA

While India Inc. has found a place on the High Table with the global business leaders and powerful MNCs, and the Indian government wants a permanent seat in the powerful most body of the UN, namely, the Security Council, they are constantly reminded that on the Human

Development Index India ranks among the most devastated economies and polities of the world. The dizzy rise of share market or the GDP growth figures make it all the more stark that the bulk of India's population lives in grovelling poverty under sub-human conditions because of callous government policies. Both the state and the central governments are often caught colluding with the rich and powerful to rob the poor of their land and other natural resources. The corporate leaders are often in the news for their unethical dealings and humungous scams. The inability of the Indian state to protect the basic human rights of its people, the absence of basic civil amenities and survival needs—such as clean drinking water, access to basic health care and education, lack of adequate food and nourishment—allow the negative stereotypes about India to abound in international media, among 'development experts' as well as in the social science discourse. For example, an international poll of 213 gender experts from five continents conducted by the Thomson-Reuters Foundation, India occupied the fourth place after Afghanistan, Congo and Pakistan in the list of the world's most dangerous countries for women. While both the methodology as well as the intent of this survey is dubious, the fact that the report was covered extensively by international media shows that the negative stereotyping of India even to the point of caricature is still far more pervasive than the positive image created by India Inc.

This is in part because our elites are by and large still working in the copycat mode. They measure their success by how effective they are in competing with the West and how well they perform when Western businesses outsource their work to them. The design as well as the ground rules of the economic game to be played is still being charted out by the West. Barring stray exceptions, the world does not see them or the Government of India display any grand vision for India's people as a whole.

THE DOMINANCE OF ENGLISH AND ANGREZIAT

One of the important reasons for the growing intellectual and emotional disconnect between the educated elites and the rest of society is that the political leaders who inherited power from the British chose to retain English as the language of administration, judiciary and elite education and profession. This dual system of education has given the educated elites unprecedented clout and access to opportunities both at home and abroad. Though their facility with the English language enabled them to communicate with the West easily, it has taken away opportunities from the population and created serious communication hurdles with their own people.

Much of the 'deprivation' suffered by certain caste groups in society is intimately linked to the loss of opportunities and honour for the bearers of traditional knowledge because it is not expressed in the English language. They are not poor because they are unemployed or unemployable. They were and continue to be productive classes of our society. What they produce is readily consumed in the national and international market. For example, our weavers produce fabrics which have been the envy of the world for centuries. Our craftsmen produce jewellery, icons and art objects that are unparalleled in beauty of design and exquisite workmanship. The children of our traditional *sthapathis* who inherited the skills required to design and make architectural wonders like the Konarak Sun Temple, the Jantar Mantar, the beautiful ancient temples, havelis and palaces found in every corner of India made with environment friendly materials found no place in modern colleges of architecture. In fact, the right to build even ordinary houses was snatched away from them because they are unable to acquire the required degrees in the English medium courses where students only learn to copy western architecture. *Sthapathis* have been degraded to the level of masons, *mistris*, and labourers at the lowest rung of our building industry. Likewise, many of our farmers have better practical knowledge of botany, seed development, genetic engineering of plants and soil conditions than many of those who are employed as agricultural scientists. They are good at reading weather forecasts from observing the changing moods of nature, often more accurately than our modern-day scientists. Their knowledge of food storage, soil conservation, use of safe pesticides, biodiversity and medicinal values of plants has till recently had hardly any takers in the scientific establishment because they could not write research papers in English. People of Prajapati

(*Kumhar*) castes who specialized in building wells, ponds and other water harvesting structures have intimate knowledge of where to build dams or bridges. Persons from such a caste background would have had far greater advantage in becoming modern-day hydraulic engineers, soil conservationists if they were given the opportunity to study modern engineering or soil conservation in their mother tongue. To add insult to injury, all of India's productive classes—weavers of exotic silks, metal workers who produce great art objects, traditional architects, jewellery makers and farmers—have been dubbed as 'backward castes' and classes all because the knowledge they represent is not acquired from text books written in English and they do not have the English education necessary for 'studying' today's science and technology books.

One cannot get entry into a 'modern' course in medicine, architecture, law, engineering or apply for even a clerical job without knowledge of English. Consequently, only the poor who cannot afford English medium education through private schools end up studying in the language of their region. Since the quality of education in government schools where children from poorer strata study is abysmally poor, most of the products of such institutions are mal-educated and hence not equipped to compete in the world of opportunities being created in the new economy, except as menials. The dual system of education—high-quality English medium education in expensive private schools for the elite and low-grade government-run schools in regional languages for the masses—has made our society resemble a headless body with the head trying to function without any connection to the body. It is a great pity that even after India was formally freed from colonial rule, we have ensured that the schism that was deliberately created by our colonial rulers between the English-educated elite and the rest of the society has grown even further and acquired deadly dimensions that are destroying the minds, souls and self-respect of the majority of our people. The edge that English-based education provides often trumps the traditional divides of caste and class.

Most educated people have come to consider this state of affairs as so 'normal' that this is not even seen as a matter of note, concern or alarm. However, the absurdity and injustice of this situation becomes obvious if we look around and observe the fact that there are not many other countries in the world where people suffer such severe deprivation and disability within their own motherland for having failed to acquire education in a foreign language.

The tiny English-speaking pan-Indian elite lacks social and cultural roots in Indian society, and their lifestyle and aspirations are directed towards the Western world, and thus lack the competence to govern a society as diverse and complex as ours. That is why the laws they enact, including those for the ostensible benefit of the people, are observed only in their violation; the law and order machinery they preside over is marked by corruption, incompetence and tyranny. Because their social reform discourse is couched in an alien language and uses an alien framework, the social reform measures they propose usually create a backlash.

Consider the absurdity and injustice evidenced in the following examples:

- There are no medical or science, technology or social science journals in any of the Indian languages, including those that are spoken by millions. All technology institutions teach in English as if English is the natural language of science and technology. This is not the case in Thailand, Korea, China, Japan, Germany or France.
- It would be difficult, if not impossible, to find training manuals for plumbers, electricians or masons in Hindi, Marathi or Tamil. As a result, people who take to these occupations end up acquiring half-baked knowledge as apprentices on the job by observing the work of others or by word of mouth. The children of our impoverished farmers and artisans learn what they can by simply following traditional ways or picking up new skills by observing others.
- India is one of the very few places in the world where pharmaceutical companies do not write the names of the medicines they produce in any local language. Almost all the allopathic medicines produced in India are labelled in English; the accompanying literature about directions for use, side effects and precautions are provided only in English. Today, even the

fashionable among Ayurvedic companies label their medicines in English. Most doctors, including those who work in government offices and service low-income groups, write their prescriptions in English. Given that only a tiny per cent among the educated sections can make sense of things written in English, imagine what it means for those who are barely literate to decipher their prescriptions and understand the nature of treatment and medication prescribed to them.

- Our lawyers draft petitions in English on behalf of even those clients who do not know a word of English; court proceedings, especially at the higher levels, are all carried out in English, legal judgements are delivered in English, the laws and precedents on which those judgements are based are leftovers of British law and are written in English. Thus most people who approach the courts for justice cannot comprehend a word of what their lawyers write or say on their behalf or make sense of the verdicts passed in their favour or against them, except through the agency of their lawyers. The sense of helplessness and crippling dependence this creates is a major reason for corruption and unaccountability and for the exploitation of the poor by our legal system.

- India is the only country where no social science journal is published in any of the Indian languages. All 'eminent' historians write their histories of India in English. All 'eminent' sociologists publish their micro- and macro-level studies of Indian society in English. For those who are not well trained in handling the English language, all the new knowledge being generated about the past and present of Indian society is inaccessible.

We celebrate those who are celebrated by the West. We ignore those who are disapproved of or looked down upon the West. Today, if you ask anyone among the English-educated elite to name three good current Indian literary authors, they are likely to name the likes of Vikram Seth, Shashi Tharoor or Amitav Ghosh. Very few will name O.V. Vijayan, who is one of the best writers in Malayalam, or Vijay Tendulkar, who wrote some of the finest plays in Marathi. Why? Because these writers wrote for fellow Indians in Indian languages and won Indian literary awards, not a British or American award! They have given us profound new insights into our society and made significant literary innovations both in form and content. But we do not consider these authors as important as authors who have won a Booker Prize. Can we think of an important Chinese, Japanese, German or French writer who has never written in the language of his/her own people? Writers elsewhere get international recognition after they have been read and admired at home.

More than a century and a half after English came to be imposed as a language of governance, more than 1 per cent of our people use it as a first or second language. For the majority, even of educated Indians, English remains at best a third language. Nearly 45 per cent people live in states where Hindi is the official language while a significant percentage of people even in states like Maharashtra, Gujarat, Kashmir, Assam, Punjab, Bengal, Andhra and Orissa have a working knowledge of Hindi. And yet, the English-educated elite get outraged at the idea of Hindustani replacing English as a link language. We have likewise neglected scholarship in the classical languages of India—such as Sanskrit, Pali, Tamil and Telugu and Sharada, the classical script for Kashmiri language.

THE COSTS OF NEGLECT

The entire society is paying for this crime. A country that produced numerous architectural wonders (not just a Taj Mahal in Agra or a Konarak Temple in Orissa) is producing the ugliest dysfunctional buildings for our everyday use. We do not even know how to preserve our ancient monuments because modern architects are ignorant about the building principles used in those structures. Since our traditional technologists were taught to respect local materials, weather conditions and cultural requirements of their clientele, we also find an enormous amount of aesthetic and structural diversity in traditional architecture from one region to another. Compare a traditional home in Kerala with that in Goa, Manipur or Rajasthan and you will appreciate what a rich diversity it represents.

By contrast, the homes, shops and offices built by our 'modern' architects are identical in design and use of materials—the modest ones resemble ugly boxes and posh ones are carbon copies of Western homes and offices. Our modern architects functioning with borrowed knowledge make unliveable and ugly buildings and homes. Our modern offices need to use artificial lights even in broad daylight in a country where sunshine is abundant. There is no provision for ventilation, with windows sealed for air conditioning in a country where power breakdown is a daily occurrence. Temples and houses made by our traditional *sthapathis* have withstood the ravages of centuries. Even as ruins they look aesthetic and grand.

The hold of mental slavery becomes evident when we consider how our modern educated town planners have fouled up all our water sources by copying the Western model of sewerage system. For centuries, human waste has been used for making agricultural manure. But through Western education we learnt to spend millions and billions of rupees in laying underground sewers, which carry human excreta and other wastes to be poured into rivers and lakes. Traditionally, we were taught to revere rivers as sacred with a rich mythology to encourage reverence towards these vital life-giving sources. Today, the sacred Ganga, Yamuna and all other rivers are so polluted that their waters have become sources of death and disease. Most of our rivers are totally dead because fish and other aquatic life cannot survive in them, leave alone procreate. Today, polluted water is the biggest cause of disease and death in our country. Almost 80 per cent of child deaths are caused due to water borne infections. The educated elite has become intellectually timid due to their awe of the West, even forgetting that urban centres in ancient and medieval India had well-developed drainage and waste disposal systems. If we want to be true innovators, we have to combine our inherited wisdom and knowledge with new skills. Gandhiji did precisely that when he developed simple but efficient dry latrines, which required very little water and effort to keep clean. In addition, these latrines have the advantage of locally recycling all of human waste matter into energy, thus, alleviating fuel and fertilizer shortage. Yet, the value of this system will be recognized only after London or Paris suburbs decide to adopt it.

BOLLYWOOD AS BRIDGE BUILDER AND CULTURAL AMBASSADOR

More than any other agency in India, Bollywood has played a vital role in building bridges of communication across class, language, regional, regional, caste and rural–urban divide. It has demonstrated through its own example that Hindustani is the most efficient link language, not just for the diverse people of India but also for neighbouring countries in the subcontinent. The vibrancy of regional language cinema also shows that the two can not only coexist very happily but also gain from each other.

Even though the bulk of Bombay films are family melodramas, they play a vital role in shaping both individual and collective aspirations regarding India's 'uniqueness' in the fast globalizing world. They have consciously worked to build a social consensus on traditions and values that need to be upheld and preserved. They are equally preoccupied with consolidating social opinion against those aspects of our cultural heritage that need to be overcome and discarded, and both these tasks are seen as essential prerequisites for India to live up to its tryst with destiny.

The Bombay film industry produces around 900 films a year—more popular entertainment than any other film centre in the world. This is the only film industry with an international reach that offers Hollywood films stiff competition in an increasing number of markets. People in almost all non-European countries are consuming Bollywood masalas (spicy melodramas) with enthusiasm.

And yet, unlike Hollywood, Bollywood did not start off with global aspirations. Hollywood spends an enormous amount of money and effort capturing world markets. Bollywood could never afford that kind of international outreach, yet its films have till very recently travelled far and wide on little more than word-of-mouth publicity. Their emotional appeal internationally is particularly astonishing, given their overwhelmingly Indic worldview. The TV networks in Indonesia, Singapore, Malaysia, Thailand, Egypt, Algeria, Morocco, the Middle East and many other Afro-Asian countries provide a staple diet of Indian cinema; often a single TV channel offers half a dozen Bollywood films per day. On the theatre circuits, audiences come to see the same Bollywood films again and again. Bollywood has conquered the hearts and minds of people even in those countries whose governments have long been hostile to India, such as Pakistan.

In Afghanistan, after the fall of the Taliban, one of the first acts of celebration noticed by the media was the sight of people queuing up outside cinema halls to see Bombay films. The common people in Muslim societies embrace Bollywood films warmly, even though some Muslim fundamentalist leaders do occasionally express hostility to the 'corrupting' influence of Hindustani films. The success of Bollywood's messages in winning the spontaneous affection of such a wide diversity of people has a valuable lesson for all those countries that are struggling to evolve into harmonious multi-ethnic societies, including Western democracies, which are confronting for the first time in their history the challenging task of absorbing vast numbers of non-European people of diverse races and religions as immigrants or fellow citizens.

THE NEW MORAL CUSTODIAN

An important reason for this enduring resonance of Bollywood is that the two great epics of India, the Ramayana and the Mahabharata, which are also the two foundational texts of the Indic civilization, have provided a very widely acceptable base for the artistic development of Indian commercial cinema. Every language group and region of India has produced its own versions of these great epics. So their appeal cuts across caste, class and regional divides. They are often critiqued, their values challenged, even parodied—but the stories within stories of these great epics remain the foundational discourse of Bombay cinema. The worldview they propagate and the values they uphold have proved remarkably resilient despite pressures for change.

Bollywood cinema has assumed the mantle of upholding a distinct moral code, just as the *pauranic kathas* once did. Indian cinema was in its infancy when the Mahatma Gandhi-led national movement was at its peak; unsurprisingly, most of our Bollywood directors and screenplay writers were deeply influenced by the Gandhian worldview. Many of them consciously and deliberately made their films a vehicle for carrying messages of social reform. Films upon films have dealt obsessively with several key components of Gandhi's social concerns, including (to name just a few): the oppression of women in family and society (*Dil Ek Mandir, Astha, Mrityudand, Nikaah*); caste-based inequalities (*Sujata, Acchut Kanya, Haasil*); the sad plight of farmers (*Do Bigha Zameen, Mother India, Ganga Jamuna*); communal prejudice (*Dharmaputra, Chhalia, Zakhm, Krantiveer*) and the divide between the rich and the poor (*Pyaasa, Lawaaris, Namak Haram, Jaagte Raho, Ameer Gharib*).

HAPPY MIX OF TRADITIONAL AND MODERN

Bombay films have become the staple emotional diet of people in many societies that are getting 'Westernized' and 'modernized' without being comfortable about it. They are popular as they always attempt to resolve conflicts and present a world where a happy balance is possible—provided 'eternal' core values are intact, which help maintaining a healthy, creative relationship with tradition while adopting modernity in appropriate doses. The success of Bollywood lies in its offering a viable alternative to a narcissistic variety of individualism that often comes with Westernization. People in non-Western cultures feel threatened by this kind of individualism because it undermines traditional institutions, especially the institution of the family.

Bollywood frowns upon mindless modernity even as it vigorously endorses an appropriate dose of it. Likewise, respect for tradition is applauded, while slavish adherence to it is disapproved of and even ridiculed. This echoes Mahatma Gandhi's advice: "It is good to swim in the waters of tradition, but to sink in them is suicide."[1] Bollywood tries to show how to swim in the waters of both tradition and modernity.

Bollywood has been as steadfast in dealing with inter-generational conflicts in values and aspirations. Our filmmakers are obsessed with resolving such conflicts in a way that leads to greater understanding and harmony in the larger family rather than a breakdown or nuclearization of it. Young people are encouraged to revolt against parental tyranny but not to disown responsibility for the care and respect due their parents and other elders.

Bollywood has conveyed this message with untiring zeal and consistency: a happy and stable family is the bedrock of our civilization, a family cannot be stable if it is a site of oppression and injustice. While our films have been obsessive in teaching young people the value of sacrifice, commitment to family well-being and respect for elders, they have been no less steadfast in telling parents and other elders that they have to earn the respect of young people by understanding their aspirations and the demands of changing times.

BREAKING ROLE RESTRICTIONS

Bollywood depicts Indian families in all permutations and combinations. There are those in which some women are the domineering matriarchs (for example, Deena Pathak in *Khubsurat*) and those where women have little or no say and are brutally oppressed (as with Raveena Tandon's character in *Daman*). We see wronged daughters-in-law as well as those who become tyrants for the whole family; there are domineering mothers-in-law who ruin the lives of their daughters-in-law, and also those who protect their bahus even against their own sons' tyranny or caprice, as in *Biwi No.1*.

It is Bollywood that gets the world to see that Indian culture allows for a whole diversity of roles and personae for a woman: a much larger range than is available in the writings of social historians and journalists. A woman can choose to be a steadfast spouse like Sita, or a besotted lover like Radha, who throws all social restraints to the winds, or a fearless, awe-inspiring Durga. She could be a Rani Roopmati or a Rani Jhansi. She could be a Mirabai or an Indira Gandhi. It is through our films that the message is communicated that an Indian woman's role in life is not to suffer indignities and tolerate injustice, that it is in her to rise like Durga and destroy evil, that such a Durga-like woman is not despised for her strength but revered, even by men. Even if she chooses to be a devoted and long-suffering wife, Bollywood is often at pains to point out that this is not because suffering is a woman's fate, but because she wishes to be the instrument of reform of unreasonable and tyrannical members of her family. We see Sita-like wives assume Chandi *roop* and stand up against wrong doers, even if that involves challenging their own husbands—as does Madhuri Dikshit in *Mrityudand* in a memorable confrontation with her husband, when she deals him the stunning verbal blow: "*Aap pati hain, parmeshwar banne ki koshish mat kijiye!*" (You are a husband, please do not try to play God).[2]

UNDOING STOCK PERCEPTIONS

Bollywood keeps transmitting this message with perseverance: a woman need not be frozen into a stereotype. It is through Bollywood films that people are told that Indian women are able to assert their rights without leading to a breakdown of families; that every woman desirous of the recognition of her selfhood does not have to walk out of her home in order to win freedom; that a woman can win everyone over to her point of view rather than be despised for her assertiveness. In the few cases where a woman feels that her well-being lies in walking out of her home like Ibsen's Nora, Bollywood invariably puts a firm stamp of approval on her choice, rather than condemn her (for instance, *Astitva* and *Arth*).

In most academic tracts and studies, Indian men are projected as cruel patriarchs who are insensitive to the needs of women and subject them to all kinds of oppression and misery. Bollywood goes beyond this simplistic stereotype and shows the soft and sentimental side of the Indian male as well. It sends a clear message to the world—a good man must be a devoted son, a doting brother, a caring husband and a good father who puts the happiness and interests of his children above his own. The Bollywood hero may be a great doctor or a feared dacoit, a gangster or an upright police officer, a Gandhian social reformer or a feudal aristocrat, but he is qualified as a hero by his family values, particularly with regard to his female relatives.

AN AFFECTIONATE PLURALISM

For newspaper-reading intellectuals across the world, India is often closely associated with recurring communal riots and ethnic strife between Hindus and Muslims, Christians and Sikhs. However, in the minds of ordinary people in societies, usually non-European, where the idea of India has been shaped by Bollywood hits, India is seen as a place where an incredibly large spectrum of diverse religious, linguistic and ethnic castes and communities coexist, bonded by a deep affection and making a respectful space for each other's unique cultural and religious identities. Film after film has obsessively emphasized the quintessential oneness of people of diverse faiths—be they Hindus, Muslims, Christians or Sikhs—and has shown them as cherishing their close ties as neighbours, friends, colleagues and fellow citizens.

The positive and often romantic portrayal of non-Hindu religious minorities in Indian films is another major reason for their international popularity. Bollywood has shown the world how people of different faiths joyfully celebrate each other's festivals, lay down their lives to protect each other and share in each other's joys, griefs and family secrets. The theme song of the film *Dhool ka Phool* made in the late 1950s: *Na tu Hindu banega na Musalman banega, insaan ki aulad hai, insaan banega* (You should grow up to be neither Hindu nor Muslim, you are the child of a human being and should remain a human being),[3] echoes the sentiment of *bhakt* Kabir. This sentiment has been repeated in film after film, strengthening the message that all are sons and daughters of Mother India are therefore inseparable, no matter how hard the politicians try to break their unity and sense of oneness.

The Sikhs are invariably depicted as generous, jovial, sincere people—always ready to help. They are portrayed as men of raw courage and willingness to take great risks for their friends and neighbours. Indian Christians are presented as God-fearing, simple people. Christian priests are invariably depicted as kind-hearted providers of charity, help and shelter to those in need. A repeated popular device for portraying Muslims as no less, if not in fact more, patriotic than Hindus is to depict them in roles of great responsibility, taking on anti-national elements and defending village, ethnic or national solidarity. For example, a film made to honour the martyrs of the Kargil war—*Maa Tujhe Salaam*—opens with a young Muslim army officer being put in charge of the most sensitive border post along the Indo-Pak border. To convey the idea that religion does not divide them he proclaims: "Our *mazhab* may be different, but our *mulk* is the same."[4]

OF DEITIES AND DEVOTEES

Bollywood as the most effective cultural ambassador of India has also kept people reminded that in the Indic worldview there is no sharp dividing line between the human and the divine. In the Indic civilization, gods and goddesses assume their human avatars and descend to earth to live the lives of ordinary men and women—sharing their joys, sorrows, trials and tribulations. In their human incarnations, the very same yardstick is used to judge them that human beings apply to each other. If Krishna, as the avatar of Vishnu, plays naughty pranks as a child, his mother has the right to give him a good thrashing. If, as an adolescent, he harasses young *gopis* and village women, they too take him to task in their own ways. When Bhagwan Ram treats his devoted wife Sita unjustly, ordinary people have the right to criticize his unfair actions and the freedom to script their own versions of the Ramayana which depict him acting more honourably than he did in the original Ramayana created by sage Valmiki.

In other words, it is Bollywood, more than any other cultural source, which has resisted the attempts of some of our inferiority complex ridden netas to make our gods and goddesses above criticism and reinterpretation. Bollywood keeps reminding people that even the gods are not to be credited with perfection. It is for devotees to demand and ensure improved behaviour every time gods make errors of judgement or act too whimsically. In film after film, we are shown a devotee who chastises a favoured deity for allowing evil people an upper hand in life or permitting injustice to thrive. And the *ishtdev* or *devi* is expected to respond to the chastisement and come to the aid of the devotee in times of need. This aid might come through the agency of a human, an animal or even a reptile. Dogs, horses, birds and even snakes are depicted in our films as active players coming to the aid of human beings who, like Draupadi, appeal for divine intervention. Such interplay should not be dismissed as mere gimmicks. It carries the important message that Indic gods are not distant creatures. They are willing to be at the beck and call of devotees who reach out for their deities as they would for close relatives in times of stress. This happens not only in popular mythologicals like *Jai Bhawani* or *Shiv Puran*, but in countless other films with more secular themes, where the personal deity constantly comes to the aid of the supplicant devotee and defeats the evil designs of all those who seek to harass him/her.

Even in this film, the purpose is not to show the victory of the Divine will over the human, but the need for humility and graceful acceptance of the inscrutable way each person's destiny unfolds for him/her. The message is that no matter how powerful or wealthy one may be, you cannot play god with either your own fate or your children's destiny.

TO SUM UP

Since the liberalism and pluralism of Bollywood is not a copycat version of Western liberalism with its unbridled individualism, Bollywood has succeeded in creating a shared cultural and emotional space for the rich and the poor, educated elites and illiterate people alike. Bollywood's nationalism is neither phobic nor parochial. Bollywood also keeps reminding our elites that their 'Made in India' heart needs to identify with and feel for their unprivileged and marginalized fellow citizens.

NOTES AND REFERENCES

1. Mahatma Gandhi, *Navajivan*, 28 June 1925, Vol. XXVII, 308.
2. Prakash Jha Productions, *Mrityudand* (1997).
3. Directed by Yash Chopra under B.R. Chopra banner, *Dhool ka Phool* (1959).
4. Directed by Tinu Varma, Production house, Mahender Dhariwal, *Maa Tujhe Salaam* (2002).

9

Conceptualizing India—The Given and the Borrowed

Kapil Kapoor

Bharatavarsha is a definite, well-defined entity in India's textual traditions and in the texts of other nations such as the Greek, the Romans, the Arabs and the Chinese. The Vishnu Purana describes the geography of this land and the people who inhabit it—so does Mahabharata. The Atharva Veda describes this entity as a cultural unit. The *Arthasastra* describes its features and its practices and its institutions as a polity. The recurrent concept of *aswamedha* also structures India as a community. The epics and the lyrical poetry such as *Meghaduta* and *Raghuvansha* draw its boundaries and evoke its soul. A particular conception of India emerges from these textual traditions and this has sedimented into the lived life of the people. This is the vision of *cakravarti kshetra*, a plural, harmonious cultural-geographic polity threaded by transcendental, synthesizing thought systems. This is the Given. The Given is now in conflict with the Borrowed, a structure based on basically the nineteenth century European conception of a 'nation' and the nineteenth century notions of 'democracy' and 'liberalism' inflected by the twentieth century 'socialism'. This Borrowed frame fails to explain the continued existence of India as one of oldest polities. But the Hindus, the carriers of this civilization for several millennia, are now afflicted by self-doubt verging on self-hate and the sea of this civilization has now receded and is being encroached upon in its own homeland. What the future holds is worthy of reflection.

We are a self-reflecting people, a reflexive culture, perhaps the only one. One is not aware of any other culture's thinkers or texts talking in third person about the 'entity' to which they belong. They may describe, as geographers, the land they inhabit or/and describe the boundaries as conquerors or empire builders, but, and one is subject to correction, there is no other instance of a people who go beyond geography and constitute in their consciousness the land they inhabit as a 'mother'.

To understand this, we have to bank on our own untranslatable vocabulary of thought. Our culture is in fact a culture of introversion—*antarmukhi*—for no entity can commonly or collectively be owned in one given way by millions of people over several millennia unless there was and has been a unity of consciousness, an inner unity, *antas ka ekatva*, a consciousness constructed over millennia by a shared lived experience, a consciousness born of some fundamental truth of experience, a *shashavata anubhuti*, that no defeat in the battlefield, no slaughter, no terror has been able to extinguish completely. It is the Hindu consciousness of this land as a mother, a sacred space, *punya bhoomi*.

This unity of consciousness is not, has not been, a product of political thought or boundaries or power exercised over others but a shared cognition of the self of a whole people, a self that is the product of a long common intellectual and emotional lived experience that has been stored in the *smrti*, mind, of an essentially oral culture. This *ekatmata* (one common self) manifests in the Hindu reverence, *shradha*, for: (*a*) the land, *bhumi*; (*b*) *devi–devata*, gods and goddesses; (*c*) dharma, the principle of righteousness and ordained duty in all matters; (*d*) *rishi-muni*, thinkers and sages; (*e*) *jivan-mulya*, values[1] that make collective and individual life harmonious and happy; (*f*) sacred spaces and places,[2] *tirthas*; (*g*) *sanskriti*, culture (literature, Veda–Purana and art, *murti–mandir*) and (*h*) *jivana-darsana*, philosophy of life that holds the happiness of all as more important than individual comfort, *sukha* not *suvidha*.

This is the 'structure of feeling' (Raymond Williams' phrase from his book *Culture and Society*)[3] shared by Hindustanis and Bharatavasis but not necessarily by all the 'educated' urban Indians. Education and a thousand years' history of vandalism and defeat in the battle fields has fragmented the Hindu self and afflicted it with self-doubt. Indian mainstream education has played from the very inception of school education in the 1930s of the nineteenth century, and continues to play this disaffiliating role. Consider this from a letter written by Lord Macaulay from Calcutta on 12 October 1836 to his father Mr Zachary Macaulay:

Our English schools are flourishing wonderfully. We find it difficult, indeed, in some places impossible, to provide instruction for all who want it. At the single town of Hoogly fourteen hundred boys are learning English. The effect of this education on the Hindoos is prodigious. No Hindoo, who has received an English education, ever remains sincerely attached to his religion. Some continue to profess it as a matter of policy; but many profess pure deism and some embrace Christianity. It is my firm belief that, if our plans are followed up, there will not be a single idolator among the respectable classes in Bengal thirty years hence. And this will be effected without any efforts to proselytize, without the smallest interference with religious liberty; merely by the natural operation of knowledge and reflection. I heartily rejoice in the prospect.[4]

A thousand years of ruthless, unmitigated violence and grief, somewhat of the kind that the Jews as a people have been subjected to throughout their history and alluded to in The Old Testament Books of Job and Joel, the traumatic destruction of Hindu communal life, monuments and institutions and the breakdown of traditional values under the impact of slaughters and wars constructed the frame of mind of a persecuted and a hounded people and the foundations of 'self-hate', a self-hate that is characteristic of all peoples who have a prolonged experience of religious, cultural persecution at the hands of an oppressor group. This new English education completed the story imposing a three-way split on the Hindu personality—those who are Hindus inside the home but anti-Hindu outside, those who are anti-Hindu both inside and outside the home and those few who are Hindus both inside and outside the home. But all the three lost their voice, their vocabulary.

The introduction of English studies has had far-reaching consequences on the Indian society and mind. On the positive side, it facilitated an interaction both with contemporary Western thought and enabled the founding of new civilizational institutions—the post office, the railways, the macadam road, the public hospitals and the municipality. There was so much visible change in Indian life and it made so much difference to the external, material conditions that the young Indian already having lost faith in himself and completely sold now on working for comfort and for good life was swept off his feet and filled with deep admiration for the West. The new thought also ushered in the much-needed social reform and many Indians distinguished themselves by introducing reform in the Hindu society and pulling it out of its defensively frozen mind. But on the flip side, the astounding material values of Western thought bedazzled the educated Indian mind so thoroughly that it ended up as a docile and dependent 'translated mind'. This subordination of the Indian mind created a de-intellectualized community completely in disjunction with its own thought and its own self and has continued to produce young people who at best are ignorant and at worst have contempt for the Indian self. And the Indian 'intellectual' is often compared by common Indians to a broiler—good to look at, brought up on a special diet but unable to stand on its own legs. These products infest the universities, fill the political class, the bureaucracy and the media are at best ignorant and at worst have contempt for them.

Therefore, India speaks in two voices and has two self-images—the Given that is shared by the vast populace and the other which is Borrowed by some of the educated class from contemporary Western liberal humanist utilitarian ethos. The Given is a Hindu consciousness and the Borrowed is the voice of those hostile to or alienated from the dominant Hindu culture of this country and include proselytizers, Marxist intellectuals, fundamentalist Islamists, power-seeking opportunist Hindus and that large segment of Indian population who subscribe to other cultures without being actually hostile to Hindu culture. It is important to note that the dichotomy is not Hindus and non-Hindus.

Indians themselves therefore have more than one image of India. When we talk of the Given, we focus on the dominant community's image of this country. And when we talk of the Borrowed, we talk of how some of us see ourselves and how the others see us. From the evidence of random records that are available in the form of travelogues and traveller's accounts and the accounts of medieval Muslim historians and the imperialist European scholars, we note that there is no one static image of how others see us. It has been changing over time but by and large, barring some of the contemporary Western critics, primarily sociologists, the others have eulogized this country, its people and the conditions of life here. Therefore, for a large segment of known history, the 'other' image has not been at variance with our Given image.

The Given is attested by an almost uninterrupted textual tradition. In this age of deliberate half truths and profitable self-flagellation when every 'educated Indian'[5] is busy denigrating his culture and traditions and everyone seems to be afflicted by a demeaning self-doubt, it is refreshing, and revelatory, to recall what this textual tradition attests about our multi-millennia old thought processes. India has been a knowledge society from the very beginning. We have the world's oldest poetry (Rig Veda), the world's oldest prose (Brahmanas), the world's oldest technical literature (Pratishakhyas) and the world's largest body of intellectual and imaginative literature in Sanskrit, Classical Tamil, Pali and Prakrit that is also among the world's earliest. Our polity is older than that of Babylonia. We have the world's first book on statecraft, Kautilya's *Arthasastra* (fourth century BC), the first book on prosody, the world's first grammar of a human language, Panini's *Ashtadhyayi* (seventh century BC) and the world's first text of interpretation, Yaska's *Nirukta* (ninth century BC), to count a few peaks.

No wonder that the learned Alberuni[6] talks with much puzzlement and some impatience of arrogant Hindus who think no end of their country and knowledge:

> We can only say, folly is an illness for which there is no medicine, and the Hindus believe that there is no country but theirs, no nation like theirs, no kings like theirs, no religion like theirs, no science like theirs. They are haughty, foolishly vain, self-conceited, and stolid. They are by nature niggardly in communicating that which they know, and they take the greatest possible care to withhold it from men of another caste among their own people, still much more, of course from any foreigner. According to their belief, there is no other country on earth but theirs, no others race of many but theirs, and no created beings besides them have any knowledge or science whatsoever. Their haughtiness is such that, if you tell them of any science or scholar in Khurasan and Persis, they will think you to be both an ignoramus and a liar.[7]

Alberuni was not exactly sympathetic. But 500 years before him, the Syrian astronomer-monk, Severus Sebokht, writing in AD 662 said:

> I shall now speak of the knowledge of the Hindus ... of their subtle discoveries in the science of Astronomy—discoveries even more ingenious

than those of the Greeks and Babylonians—of their rational system of Mathematics, or of their method of calculation which no words can praise enough—I mean the system of nine symbols.[8]

Let us go further back and to another people and juxtapose with contemporary rubbishing of Hindus for lacking the principle of equality what around first century CE. Diodorus Siculus of Sicily avers about the Hindu social–political practices. Sri V.S. Agrawala in his celebrated book *India as Known to Panini* presents a tantalizing passage in Diodorus Siculus[9] which seems to be derived from Megasthenes:

Of several remarkable customs existing among the Indians, there is one prescribed by their [sc. Indian] ancient philosophers which one may regard as truly admirable: for the law ordains that no one among them shall, under any circumstances, be a slave, but that, enjoying freedom, they shall respect the principle of equality in all persons: for those, they thought, who have learned neither to domineer over nor to cringe to others will attain the life best adapted for all vicissitudes of lot: since it is silly to make laws on the basis of equality of all persons and yet to establish inequalities in social intercourse.[10]

Contrast this with the social divisions accepted as a part of the state at the very roots of Western civilization, including slavery, a practice that lasted till as recent times as mid-nineteenth century when the American Civil War was waged to free the black slaves. Aristotle in his *Politics* notes:

But then to inquire into the essence and attributes of various kinds of governance first of all we must determine 'What is a State?' State is a community made of several elements—these elements, according to Aristotle, are: "... the food producing class...; the class of mechanics who practice the crafts without which a city [read State] can not exist.... The third class is that of the traders ... engaged in buying and selling. A fourth class is that of serfs or labourers. The warriors make up the fifth class.... The higher parts of the State, say, the warrior class ... engaged in the administration of justice, and that engaged in deliberation ... these are more essential to the State than the parts that minister to the necessaries of life.... The higher as well as the lower elements are to be equally considered parts of the State."[11]

We cannot miss that these are professional classes and very much like the *varna*s of Hindu society, accept that the Hindus proscribed slavery. It is another matter that for hundreds of years, they were captured and sold as slaves in the central Asian markets.

And representation has to be distributed taking into account the fact that 'education and virtue have superior claims'.[12] And people are free to choose as liberty is the condition of justice.[13] This 'polity' of Aristotle, a form of government that combines virtue with voice, is the one that had been practiced in Hindu society and states, a form of government with dharma as the one word unwritten constitution before Islamic conquests from twelfth century onwards disrupted the system by substituting 'power' for dharma. Here is an account of the lived life of the people by the sixth century Chinese traveller Hiuen Tsiang who, besides giving interesting vignettes of life, reaffirms what Diodorus Siculus said that among these people there is no forced labour or slavery:

> Hiuen-Tsiang speaks of the common people in the highest terms: ... they are volatile, but "gentle and sweet, straight-forward, honourable, keeping their word, with no fraud, treachery or deceit about them." criminals are rare, and these few are not even beaten, and are never put to death, but cast into prison and left to live or die, "not being counted among men." A small payment is exacted for a small offence; but those who seriously offend the moral sense of the community are mutilated in various ways, or expelled from it.[14]

We are next told of etiquette and are informed that no less than nine ways of being polite are employed. Of these, the most respectful is to cast one's self on the ground, and then to kneel "and laud the virtues of the one you address" [...] "The honourable person ... reverenced must speak gently to the inferior, and touch his head, or pat him on the back, and give him kindly orders or good advice, in order to show affection."

When ill, there is no rush to the physic-bottle. "Every-one who falls sick, fasts for seven days. Should he not get well in the course of this period, he takes medicine." Hiuen-Tsiang causes us no surprise when he informs us that "doctors differ in their modes of treatment".

At funerals there are weepings and lamentable cries [...]. No one takes food in a house where someone has died until after the funeral;

and all who have been at the deathbed are unclean until they have bathed outside the town.

Hiuen-Tsiang speaks of the civil administration as being mild and benevolent. Officials have "a portion of land assigned to them for their personal support". There is neither registration of families nor forced labour. Rajas possess their own private domains, divided into four portions; whereof one provides for state-matters and the cost of sacrifices; one for salaries; one for rewarding men of exceptional talent; and the fourth affords charity to religious bodies […]. Taxation is light, and the personal service required is moderate, labour at public works being paid for.

The Hindu notions of state and polity, rooted as they are in geography and culture rather than ethnicity, language and religion, need annotation. The two words used are tell-tale—*desha* and *rashtra*. *Desha* stands for 'place'/'land' and *rashtra* is this land constituting a cultural entity, a unity of belief, thought, values, practices and objects of reverence. The word 'nation', a construct of nineteenth century European one language, one ethnicity, one religion political formation does not apply to India—instead of questioning the definition some of our intellectuals have questioned the very existence of India as an entity and or a period of time debated ad nauseam the question "Is India a 'Nation'" as if it has to be one in the European mould. The Hindus think in terms of their place of habitation. Moving from the whole to the part, they begin with the earth, *bhumi*, move to a part of this earth, a continent, most likely Asia, and call it *jambudvipa*. In that there is a *khanda*, part called Bharata Khanda, *jambudvipe bharatakhande*, an area which is designated as *cakravarti kshetra*, a wheel-like area with a *dhuri*, the central axle around which the 'wheel', the cultural unit, Bharatavarsha revolves. This hub is in and around Ujjain, for ages the hub of Indian intellectual, cultural and political life, a home to scientists, poets, philosophers and great emperors such as Varahamihira, Kalidasa, Bhartrhari and Vikramaditya. It is also our Greenwich—India's *kala-ganana*, time-reckoning, is based on the Tropic of Cancer that runs underneath the Mangalanath Temple, the temple dedicated to Mars on the bank of River Shipra in Ujjain.

For Hindus this *desha*, country, the land from the Himalayas to the southern sea is 'sacred', *punyabhumi*. The earth, *prithvi*, 'one that has a spread', in our textual tradition, is one of the fourteen in the universe and is designated as *vasundhara*, 'the holder of *ratna*, diamonds and other precious stones'.[15] It is referred to as 'the mother earth', *dharti mata*, in common parlance and in a major Puranika narrative, it is said that Dattatreya, a great sage, who learnt 22 lessons from various objects of nature, learnt *dhairya*, patience, from the mother earth. It is revered as a sustainer. Practicing Hindus when they get up in the morning they seek forgiveness from the mother earth before putting down their feet on it. The whole earth is sacred but just as there are some parts of the body that are more *unnata*, elevated, the part of the earth identified by our ancient geographers as *jambudvipe bharatakhande*, the land that is Bharata. Hindus, pagans that they are, visualize their country as a woman, call it Mother and revere this *bhu-bhaga*, part of the earth, as a land of plenty, of 'milk and honey' as *shasyashyamala*, ever so beautifully green, with the world's highest mountain range adorning its head and the largest ocean washing its feet, where great thinkers and sages have taken birth and which is the original home of *jnana*, knowledge, and has produced the world's largest body of intellectual literature.[16]

While the whole *Bharatakhanda* is sacred, there are sites, locations that are designated as 'sacred'. Just as the whole body is important but some limbs, the head, the right hand for example, are considered *pavitra*, pure. Fire or energy is present in every object but it quickly manifests in the matchstick, spreads faster in wood than stone,[17] and instantly appears in *karpura*. So sanctity marks the cosmos and all earth but this element of sanctity is more markedly present in some constellations and in some sites. These sites on this earth are held to be particularly 'pure' by virtue of, either their own power, *siddha sthana* (viz. Mount Kailash, the lake Manasarovar both in Tibet), or being the *tapo-bhumi* (place of action, performances and austerities) of some *rishi-muni* (an inspired sage, ascetic) (viz. Veda Vyasa in Badrikashrama), or where some mahatma (saintly great-soul) meditated and created knowledge (viz. Sharda Pitha, Sringeri, Jnaneshwara in Paithan?), or being the *lila-bhumi* ('playground') of the avatars (recurrent manifestations in human form of the immanent principle of energy, Brahman) where they enacted their life span (viz. Mathura, *janmasthana*, where Krishna was born in a jail).

The whole country is dotted with such dedicated places scattered around and across the land. Practically every village has a sacred place, a temple, forest. There are sacred forests (*aranya, vana*), areas (*kshetra*), mountains (*parvata*), water bodies, tanks (*jalashaya*), rivers (*nadiyan*), trees (*vrksha*), animals (*pashu*), birds (*pakshi*), cities (*puriyan*) and geometrical forms (*yantra*) and through them the average Hindu is linked in a chain of cosmic spirituality with all forms of life and being. Interestingly the odd numbers three, five, seven, nine and those divisible by three are auspicious in the enumeration of sacred places. There are 51 Siddha-Kshetras (geographic areas endowed with extraordinary power); 51 Shakti-Pitha (sites associated with Parvati, the consort of Shiva, and symbolizing female power and divinity); 12 *jyotirlinga*s, sites of Shiva-worship; 21 Ganapati Kshetras, sites of Ganesha worship; 32 sacred caves/cave complexes; five Natha (major forms of Vishnu in five places); seven Saraswatis (forms of the Pauranika river Saraswati); 14 *prayaga*s, confluences; seven water bodies, tanks; nine forests; seven *kshetra*s (sacred areas); seven rivers; four *dhama*; and nine cities.

In the cline of sacredness, first we have the nine sacred cities (*puriyan*)—Ayodhya, where Rama, one of the 10 avatars, was born; Mathura, the birthplace of Krishna; Kashi, the city of Shiva, one of the trinity, the god of learning, dance; Kanchi, the second eye of Shiva, one of the 51 Shakti-Pitha; Ujjain, an ancient city, one of the three where the 12-yearly Kumbha Mela is held, seat of Hindu time-reckoning and a seat of tantra philosophy; Dwaraka, one of the four most sacred *dhama*s, from where Krishna ruled and a seat of learning and Maya or Haridwar, the place where the Ganga leaves the Himalayas and enters the plains. The four *dhama*s are in the four corners of India—Badrinath in the north, Rameshwaram in the south, Dwaraka in the west and Jagannatha Puri in the east. These are the principal sites. There are secondary enumerations of places sacred to different deities, schools (*sampradaya*), Jaina and Buddhist sites and hundreds of sites associated with Pauranika narratives. This investment of land with shared associations and meanings makes it an object of reverence, worship.

Vishnupurana, first century CE, describes this country exactly as that. It enumerates:

Its dimensions:

The country that lies north of the ocean, and south of the snowy mountains, is called Bharatra, for there dwelt the descendants of

Bharata. It is nine thousand leagues in extent and is the land of works, in consequence of which men go to heaven or obtain emancipation.

Its mountains:

The seven main chains of mountains in Bharata are Mahendra, Malaya, Sahya, Suktimat, Riksha, Vindhya and Paripatra.

Its character:

From this region heaven is obtained, or even, in some cases, liberation from existence.

Its nine divisions:

The Varsha of Bharata is divided into nine portions, which I will name to you; they are Indra-dvipa, Kaserumat, Tamravarna, Gabhastimat, Naga-dvipa, Saumya, Gandharba and Varuna. On the east of Bharata dwell the Kiratas (the barbarians); on the west, the Yavanas; in the centre reside Brahmans, Kshatriyas, Vaisyas and Sudras, occupied in their respective duties of sacrifice, arms, trade and service.

Its rivers:

The Satadru, Chandrabhaga and other rivers flow from the foot of Himalaya; the Vedasmriti and others from the Paripatra mountains; the Narmada and Surasa from the Vindhya hills; the Tapi, Payoshni and Nirvindhya from the Riksha mountains; the Godavari, Bhimararthi, Krishnaveni and others from the Sahya mountains; the Kritamala, Tamraparni and others from the Malaya hills; the Trisama, Rishikulya, etc., from the Mahendra, and the Rishikulya, Kumari and others from the Suktimat mountains. Of such as these, and of minor rivers, there is an infinite number; and many nations inhabit the countries on their borders.

Its diverse people:

The principal nations of Bharata are the Kurus and Panchalas in the middle districts; the people of Kamarupa in the east; the Pundras, Kalingas, Magadhas and southern nations are in the south; in the extreme west are the Saurashtras, Suras, Bhiras, Arbudas; the Karushas and Malavas, dwelling along the Paripatra mountains; the Sauviras, the Saindhavas, the Hunas, the Salwas, the people of Sakala, the Madras, the Ramas, the Ambashthas and the Parasikas, etc. These nations drink of the water of the rivers above enumerated and inhabit their borders, happy and prosperous.

Its knowledge and asceticism:

In the Bharatavarsha it is that the succession of four Yugas, or ages, the Krita, the Treta, the Dvapara and Kali, takes place; that pious ascetics engage in rigorous penance; that devout men offer sacrifices; and that gifts are distributed; all for the sake of another world. In Jambu-dvipa, Vishnu, consisting of sacrifice, is worshipped, as the male of sacrificial rites, with sacrificial ceremonies; he is adored under other forms elsewhere.

Its distinction and difference from other lands and the blessing of being born here:

Bharata is therefore the best of the divisions of Jambu-dvipa, because it is the land of (deeds) works (*yoga-bhumi*), the others are places of enjoyment (*bhoga-bhumi*) alone. It is only after many thousand births, and the aggregation of much merit, that living beings are sometimes born in Bharata as men. The gods themselves exclaim,

> Happy are those who are born, even from the condition of gods, as men in Bharata-varsha, as that is the way to the pleasures of Paradise, or the greater blessing of final liberation. Happy are they who, consigning all the unheeded rewards of their acts to the supreme and eternal Vishnu, obtain existence in that land of works, as their path to him. We know not, when the acts that have obtained us heaven shall have been fully recompensed, where we shall renew corporeal confinement; but we know that those men are fortunate who are born with perfect faculties in Bharata-varsha.[18]

Around the time this was being composed, the Roman Ptolemy prepared a map of India:

The other Roman maps of central India show the inland river routes and paths to fabled places such as Ujjain where precious stones, emeralds, opals and rubies were in abundance. Ptolemy's two maps of north-west and central India map the sources of gems. The text *Periplus of the Erythraean Seas*, first century AD, describes the maritime trade in

Figure 9.1: Ptolemy's Third Century Map of India

what is known today as Arabian Sea and Indian Ocean and mentions three Indian ports for picking up precious stones—Barbarike in the Indus estuary from where the exports included turquoise and lapis lazuli; Barugaza (modern Broach, Gujarat, India) at the mouth of the Narmada River where the Romans bought onyx stones mined from the old beds of the Narmada; Muziris on the south-west coast of India from diamonds, sapphires and pearls were exported.[19]

Evidently, cartography is an imperialist and trading instrument. India has enormous geographic knowledge of India and Asia in texts such as Rig Veda and Puranas.[20] But India never drew maps of other countries, nor did we search for routes and paths because our country has all and all kinds of wealth—from food to diamonds and gold to knowledge. We never needed to go out for anything—so we were neither travellers nor imperialists. Armies never marched out of India—ideas, thought did. But the consciousness that this needs to be defended is an ancient consciousness. In the Prithvisukta of *Atharvaveda*, there is a prayer—"O mother earth destroy those who want to subdue my *rashtra* by *shastra*, weapons, or *shastra*, ideas." Beginning with Islamic invasions, India was subdued by weapons and beginning with the British, India has been subdued by ideas, a deeper tragedy.

But after the Islamic destruction, there is a watershed. We lost faith in ourselves and our culture and tradition came face to face with annihilation. The sea of Hindu faith that once spread from Iraq to the West to Central Asia and East and South East Asia started receding with the loss and defeat after deadly struggles of the Hindu kingdoms of Gandhara, Kapisa, Peshawar, Multan and Kashmir. The narrative of Hindu resistance has not yet been told in full detail—it is a gory tale of valour and disaster. Today Hinduism is under siege in its own heartland with numerous forces working to de-Hinduize the country and the Hindus themselves, suffering from self-hate and victims of Stockholm syndrome, colluding in the destruction of their own self. Hindus are in a suicidal mode. Our early medieval texts, Puranas[21] saw the danger, warned against it, asked questions and suggested remedies—but not of much avail.

The *Skandapurana*, after Prithviraj Chauhan's defeat at Tarain, addresses itself to the question why the Hindu kings fell one after another like nine pins before Muhammad Ghauri, who is described as the king of Lamghan who matches Indra in valour—*lamghan adhipati Mahendra sama vikramah*—and attributes it to their love of comfort, ignorant confidence and the reluctance to pursue the enemy to his home. The *Bhavishya Purana* describes the rise of *maleccha* (non-native kings), their wealth and their inherent hostility towards Bharata. It then describes the few patriotic kings who defeated them and protected dharma. In this context the Purana expresses deep sorrow over the destruction of *Bharatiya sanskriti*, the native culture and its artefacts and narrates the achievements of the revered kings and warriors such as Asoka, Chandragupta, Vikramaditya, Bhojraja, Prithviraj, Shivaji and Rana Pratap. It was evidently composed before the time of Guru Govind Singh or else the great saint-soldier, the exceptional defender of dharma too would have entered the enumeration. The country and its culture is extensively described in the great *kavya*s such as Ramayana, Mahabharata and Bhagavad Purana and in the ancient *laukika*, popular literature such as that of the dramatist Bhasa, the poets Kalidasa, Bhatti, Bhavabhuti, kshemendra, Sri Harsha and Madhava and in the medieval popular poetry—*Vidyapati, Hammirakavya, Surjanacarita, Prithviraja Raso*, etc.

This large body of literature kept the flame of love for the land and its culture alive in the hearts of ordinary people. Macaulay realized that the inner self of the people of India is deeply imbued with *rashtrabhava* and if these people are to be ruled this inner self must be transformed and his move to introduce English and the English education and link it with employment did what 800 years of violence could not achieve—as we noted above, the Hindu mind, subjugated and subordinated, lost creativity and self-respect and revelled in self-denigration. The nineteenth century saw several sociocultural movements such as Brahmo Samaj, Arya Samaj but all were shared the apparently rational critique of Hinduism and were reformist in the Christian mould and apologetic about Hindu cultural practices such as polytheism and idol-worship, the few like Ishwarchandra Vidyasagara and Vivekananda notwithstanding. This is the story with which we enter the contemporary times. There are straws in the wind and sometimes one agrees with Ulysses—'though much is lost much abides'. On that note we conclude this mini Purana.

NOTES AND REFERENCES

1. See Bhagavad Gita 16.1–3, *Caraka Samhita* 1.8.18–25 and *Yogasutra* 1.33 for some enumerations of these values.

2. As we noted in one of our lectures (Kapil Kapoor, *Importance of the Sacred in Early India*, University of Ulster, UK, 2007):

    > The principle of Sacred—Non-Sacred determines in the Hindu world-view, the propriety, the right and wrong, the desirability of all thoughts, actions and desires of the human beings and therefore is a principle connected with man and not with God or divinity. In the over-riding Hindu framework of *purusartha*, the four means towards the goal of life, righteousness, material well-being, fulfillment of desires and liberation from suffering in this mortal world, all human action is to be measured by this principle of sacredness. This centering of sacredness in the human world more than anything else marks off Hinduism from the other cultures in which sacred (from Latin, *sacer*, "untouchable") or "holy", objects, places or concepts are believed by followers to be intimately connected with God or a divinity.

3. Raymond Williams, *Culture and Society 1780–1950* (Doubleday & Company Inc., 1960).

4. *Selections From Macaulay Letters, Prose, Speeches and Poetry*, edited with Introduction and Notes by E.V. Downs and G.L. Davies (London: Methuen's English Classics, Methuen and Co. Ltd, 1930).

5. This is how the victims of Indian education are described, says Ananda Coomaraswamy.

6. Abu Rayhan Muhammad ibn Ahmad al-Biruni (Alberuni) (973–1048) was a Persian scholar who was active in a great variety of sciences. In particular, he was one of the first writers to produce a systematic study of Indian culture, having visited India in 1030 during the campaigns of Mahmud of Ghazni.

7. Edward C. Sachau (ed.), *Alberuni's India* (New Delhi: Indialog Publications Pvt. Ltd, 2003).

8. A.L. Basham, *The Wonder That Was India* (Picador India, Paperback Reprint, 2004). (Frontis piece of the book.)

9. See Diodorus Siculus 2.39, in R.C. Majumdar (ed.), *The Classical Accounts of India* (Calcutta: Firma K.L. Mukhopadhyaya, 1960), 236.

10. V.S. Agrawala, *India as Known to Panini* (Varanasi: Chowkhamba, 1963).

11. Aristotle, *Politics*, Chapter 4 (New York: Carlton Press).

12. Aristotle, *Politics*, III.13.

13. Aristotle, VI.2.

14. William Boulting, *Four Pilgrims* (London: K. Paul. Trench, Trubner and Co. Ltd, before 1923; New Delhi: Indian Asian Education Services, 2001, Reprint).

15. There are contending cosmologies in different Puras, texts, however, and an alternative structure would see the islands, etc., as parts of the universe, and the solar system as a *bhuvana*, a 'world', in which then this earth appears lower in the hierarchy (*Tantraloka* VIII). However, the sanctity of the whole universe is invariant.

16. Macaulay and some 'educated' Indians notwithstanding!

17. There are 10 and all are forms of Vishnu, the sustainer, suggesting that the Great Self takes human forms to sustain the human world—"To protect the good and destroy the wrong-doers, I take form again and again to re-establish righteousness"—Krishna to Arjuna in the battle field of Mahabharata (the Bhagavad Gita IV.8). The Hindus believe that in the cycle of existence, whenever there is a decline of righteousness, some great human being takes birth from age to age and the places associated with them become 'sacred'.

18. Jambudvipa Bharatakhanda Chapter III, *Vishnu Purana,* tr. H.H. Wilson, Calcutta, Punthi Pustak, 1961.

19. See Peter Francis Jr, *Indian Agate Beads,* World of Beads Monograph Series 6 (Lake Placid: Lapis Route Books, 1982). See 'Roman Maps and the Concept of Indian Gems' (The Bead Site = Home > Ancient Beads > India > Roman Maps); Peter Francis Jr, *Indian Agate* Beads; G.W.B. Huntingford, *The Periplus of the Erythraean Sea* (London: Hakluyt Society Series ii, #151, 1980); Edward Luther Stevenson, *Claudius Ptolemy The Geography* (New York: Dover Publications, 1991).

20. See Manohar Lal Bhargava, *The Geography of Rgvedic India* (Lucknow: The Upper India Publishing House Ltd, 1964); Vettam Mani, *Puranic Encyclopaedia: A Comprehensive Work with Special Reference to the Epic and Puranic Literature.* Each Purana has a geography section called *Bhuvana Kosha, Bhagavata Purana, Mtasyapurana, Brahmandapurana, Visnupurana* and *Skandapurana* have more information than other Puranas.

21. There is a convention in the composition of the Puranas. Often the composer places himself before the time and events he is narrating and talks of them in the future tense. *Bhavishya Purana* is an example.

10

India as the Other in Partition Literature

Sukrita Paul Kumar

The collective self-perception of the peoples of a nation evolves over time and acquires a position of stability through a lot of sociopolitical churning. Literature is the creative articulation of varied self-perceptions that tell the collective tale of a people. In her acclaimed novel *Aag ka Darya* (published as *The River of Fire* in English), the Urdu writer Qurratulain Hyder skilfully delineates the centuries long process of the evolution of composite culture in India. Krishna Sobti, the eminent writer in Hindi captures the early twentieth century stability and steady vibrancy of 'living together' of different communities in her classic novel *Zindaginama*. In both the novels, towards the end there are forebodings of the impending rupture of the assured stability with the shadow of Partition looming over the subcontinent.

In 1947 with the actual transfer of power to two sovereign nations in the Indian subcontinent, the euphoria of Independence could hardly be savoured amidst the barbarity of communal frenzy. With daggers drawn in an atmosphere of suspicion and fear, human beings went berserk and became captives of communal categories, killing, raping and assaulting each other and migrating to the other side of the border for life and security with a hope to come back home sometime later. In the words of Mushirul Hasan, it was as if "[t]he civilizational rhythm of the subcontinent was being irreparably destroyed".[1] That was Partition. India was cracking up. On the face of it, it was the end of an era and the beginning of another. But Radcliff's pen could in no way have clipped human consciousness with the mere drawing of borders between India and Pakistan.

People carried their old *basti*(s) (community dwellings) to new locations and their past to their present. They gradually went through the process of translation, assimilation and change to eventually evolve new stabilities and identities. By the early twentieth century, with the process of colonization by the Britishers, and thanks to the struggle for freedom from them, different states and regions were consolidated and India began to be clearly perceived as a single country, the country that sought freedom from the British. But then along with this freedom came the bloodshed of the division of this country and the dislocation of several millions of people. Carrying within themselves the shadowy borders, the brick and mortar of their homes, the gullies and lanes of their cities, the migrants on both sides of the borders also transported across their memories of sorrows and happiness, their sociology and culture.

The protagonist of Intezar Husain's Urdu novel, *Basti*,[2] Zakir, constantly mediates and modifies his past in accordance with the significance and nature of his present. Zakir teaches history and is professionally dealing and actually grappling with the linearity of time flowing uninterruptedly. Psychologically he confronts the discontinuities and ruptures juxtaposed with the images and the experiences of the past flashing on the screen of his mind. His sense of personal history calls for a fundamental rethinking about historiography. Problematizing his experience of history, he thinks:

> How boring it is teaching history to boys. Other people's history can be read comfortably, the way a novel can be read. But my own history? I'm on the run from my own history—and catching my breath in the present. Escapist. But the merciless present pushes us back again toward our history. The mind keeps talking.[3]

The stream of his consciousness oscillates between the so-called past and his present blurring all divisions of time.

The inevitable question then is, how is he going to come out of the hypnotic nostalgia of the past which presents itself to him repeatedly in the form of Roopnagar, literally meaning the city of beauty? The author could have, after all, accorded it the actual name of a city in India. But then he needed to emphasize the happy memory of the social and natural harmony of that pre-partition town through the name Roopnagar.

Partition has disrupted this harmony and ironically it is the memory of this disruption that brings him back to his now, connecting him with his present, 25 years later.

As evidenced in Rahi Masoom Raza's powerful Hindi novel *Adha Gaon*,[4] many Muslims could not quite work out and understand the logic behind Muslim nationalism. Nor did the majority of Hindus and Sikhs have any alignment with the two-nation theory. Trapped in the crossfire of hatred between the two communities in 1947, thousands fled out of their homes with no destination in mind. 'India' and 'Pakistan' were mere territorial abstractions[5] to people who had no sense of the newly demarcated frontiers. They had little knowledge of how Mountbatten's Plan or the Radcliffe Award would change the destinies of millions and tear them apart from the familial, social and cultural moorings.

In the Urdu novella, *Khwabro*[6] by Joginder Paul, Deewane Maulavi Saheb suffers from no sense of loss only because he has taken refuge in insanity. In Karachi he is thoroughly convinced of still living in Lucknow. While the locale of the novella is Karachi, it begins with the assertion "This is Lucknow …". As soon as the *mohajir*s "recovered their breath after reaching Karachi, the entire city emerged from their hearts, brick by brick".[7] In the waking hours they come to terms with the new location while in their sleep they throng to the Chowk of Ameenabad of Lucknow. To Zakir in the novel *Basti*, reality appears swathed in an eerie half-light, at times making the past more real than the present. In both the novels, the process of the assimilation of the past within the present passes through as it were a twilight zone. It is a twilight in which there are flashes of revelations, a zone in which when Roopnagar is actually totally empty, he reflects, "Yar, how strange it is that the same town becomes more meaningful for those who had to leave it".[8] For him too, Roopnagar became all the more meaningful because he had come away to Pakistan. In *Khwabro* (Sleepwalkers), Ishaq Mirza writes to Hashim projecting a similar position: "Subhan Allah! Lucknow is actually here…. Over there, we could never figure out where Lucknow had vanished from Lucknow…. Bhai, the reality of Lucknow after all lies in the elegance of Lucknow…. Actually you are the genuine Lukhnavis … settled here in your Lucknow."[9]

In both these novels, it is the second generation, Zakir in *Basti* and Ishaq Mirza in *Khwabro*, who perceive the true status of the cities from where they fled with their fathers. In his mind, Deewane Maulavi Saheb never migrated. He has forever remained in Lucknow. Nor have Zakir's father and mother for that matter. Their consciousness remains with their family heirlooms lying locked in the storeroom of their mansion in Roopnagar. They have to go and get these heirlooms before termites get to them. Zakir muses, "Is time a termite, or is a termite time?"[10] Abbajan of *Basti* and Deewane Maulavi Sahib of *Khwabro* both remain rooted, attached and static despite their migration and their sons, while Zakir and Ishaq Mirza are wanderers forever, despite their settlement in their Pakistan homes. Ishaq marries a Sindhi girl, as if announcing himself to be different: he then becomes responsible in creating another reality, the third reality born out of a past given to him by Deewane Maulavi Saheb and a present which is distinctly post-partition. *Basti* written in 1979 and *Khwabro* in 1990, so many years after the actual experience of Partition, these novels record the movement into time, across time and even beyond time. In *Basti*, says Ammi: "Oh, what does time have to do with it.... Time always goes on passing...."[11]

Though the novel *Basti* seems to cover a span of only a few months in the life of Zakir, in effect it brings into itself the cultural backdrop of centuries of Muslim history, in flashbacks. The main connectives to be found in modern history begin from 1857 and move on to 1947, and then to 1965 and finally to the 1971 disintegration of Pakistan. Gradually Roopnagar becomes a vague and distant reality with the new slogan "Crush India" coming in "like a whirlwind". India emerged as the other, getting defined through hatred, going beyond translation. While Roopnagar which also identifies with Zakir's beloved, Sabirah—who did not come away to Pakistan—the political entity called 'India' became a distant and something to be reckoned with. But then, for Roopnagar, Zakir at least has a prayer: "If something happened to this city how could I bear it?"[12]

In *Khwabro*, Deewane Maulavi Saheb actually comes out of his Lucknow in his mind in an explosion of a bomb in his haveli. But only to slip into another false belief brought out delicately in the novel: that he is in Karachi temporarily, merely on a visit, waiting to go back to his Lucknow. Not so with the grandson Salim though: "But this is Lucknow, Bade Abbu!" says the lad, running after the ball at the end of the novel. This is the Lucknow which is only a part of Karachi, a Lucknow recreated with a difference. This Lucknow includes the presence of the Sindhi cook, bringing another dimension into its culture. These are the new local dynamics of Karachi. The process of absorption, of exclusion within the politics of Pakistan on its own but of course an ongoing love–hate relationship with India.

The seeds of communalism sown and nourished by vested political interests but not very visible at the ordinary level of existence prior to Partition surfaced with an unbounded fury, capturing cities, *qasba*s and different locations alike in 1947. Kamleshwar, the well-known Hindi writer, for instance, was compelled to tell the tale of a *qasba* in UP, which came into the grip of chaos and the clutches of communal suspicion, in his novel *Laute Hue Musafir* (The Migrants Who Came Back). The novel takes the reader to the cobbler, the cycle-repairer, to the small craftsmen and the struggling youth, to their everyday, simple conversation demonstrating the faith and love existent between the Hindus and the Muslims of that small town. There is a sudden mental division of that society into Hindus and Muslims. The novel begins with the memory of almost a dream-like but real scenes of what is called Ganga–Jamuni culture, when, for instance, on the occasion of Muharrum, Taziya would pass through a Hindu locality, Hindus would sprinkle rose water on it with utmost reverence; and Muslim women came and peeped out from the *chic*s hanging on their doors to have a 'darshan', a glimpse, of Ramleela.

But after 1945, this *basti* began to simmer latently with communal feelings and gradually the bonds of love and faith in people's hearts began to collapse. Come Partition and there was an exodus by hordes of them, leaving behind Naseeban and her mud-house, the *jhopadi* amidst the debris and ruins of old houses and hutments as mere signs of former life in that *qasba*. A large group of Muslim migrants left this *basti* with the faith that they will reach Pakistan eventually. But they could not. They somehow got dispersed here and there in that zilla and did not come back lest the Hindus take offence to their return. Strangely, the Hindus too had fled because of the heavy Muslim presence in that region. Iftikar, a character in the novel perceives his fate clearly: "Even if Pakistan comes to exist, of what use will it be to us. In Pakistan, too, we will after all be ikkawallahs, pulling carts and horses."[13]

The real struggle, it is gently established, is between the rich and the poor. Though there were no live fires in that area, many a heart was consumed by the fire of hatred. All those poor migrants had no means of realizing their Pakistan. Naseeban is the lonesome witness of the desolation of the *basti*. More importantly, she is also the witness years later of the scene when grown up children of those lost migrants come back to this *basti* in search of labour. Partition had dampened and dispersed the older generation. The basti had disintegrated. With the emergence of industry and the tube wells being set up, there were prospects for employment and survival. There are some signs of development and progress and the India of this *basti* sees Naseeban smile with hope and good cheer. Naseeban's eyes twinkle and she cries with happiness: there is recognition instantly. They had come back, as the narrative emphasizes, to be housed in their homes, on this side of the border within the geopolitical entity that is India. Not as in Intezar Husain's *Basti* where "the city has already burned, but our tails are still burning".[14]

In *Laute Hue Musafir*, the children of the migrants find old homes and have new prospects. But in a sense, in *Basti* too Zakir and Afsal come 'home', even though they actually return to the graves of the older generation at the end of the novel. After this, Zakir determines to write a letter to Sabirah "before the parting of her hair fills with silver, and before the keys rust...."[15] This is in fact the moment of liberation, of moving on, connecting and rebuilding rather than remaining in the framework of the Partition psychosis existentially. Obviously, this is not easy since the politics of the country have kept the atmosphere of strife constantly alive through sporadic riots and curfews. In Karachi as in Bhiwandi, in both India and Pakistan, the legacy of Partition manifested itself in ethnic and communal tension.

In Ali Imam Naqvi's touching Urdu short story 'Dongarivari ke Gidhh' (The Vultures of the Parsi Cemetery), Hormoz and Pharoz, the two attendants in the Parsi cemetery, panic when they discover that there are no vultures that day to attend to the corpses in the cemetery that day. The police commissioner tells the board:

> 'all of them are flocking to the Kharki, Raviwar Peth and Somwar Peth, the areas where riots have broken out....' Oh those Hindus and Muslims are at each other's throats again. There's been a riot. The bastards they've

torched everything, houses, shops, even ambulances and hearses, the whole lot. The street is littered with corpses. One right on top of the other. Piled high. Our vultures ... well, they're having a field day there. And that police commissioner ... he said 'after the street's been cleaned up, the vultures will come back on their own accord.' 'Even if the street's cleaned up- so what? What makes you think the vultures will return? This fucking India ... there's a riot everyday here, everyday a fire, everyday people die. The vultures will come back?? The hell they will!'[16]

When life is thus disturbed, whether between Hindus and Muslims or through riots at Karachi because of the tension between the *mohajirs* and the 'natives', there is a continued Partition being carried through time, getting translated and expressed in poems, short and long fiction. If translation is dissemination and a metaphor for travel as well, one can find pertinent examples in Khushwant Singh's novel *A Train to Pakistan*, Krishan Chander's story 'Peshawar Express', Bhisham Sahni's short story 'Amritsar Aa Gaya' or Gulzar's story 'Khauf—these, and many stories where the train carries fear, hatred, vengefulness, sadness, bewilderment across the borders for the two nations to deal with these deep experiences down these long lanes of history.

The writer articulates different forms of ethnic and racial violence in his many-sided plurilingual writing taking place across and between languages. To what extent are the geographical spaces politically defined, how identities are determined and perceived, what conceptual formulations may be at work in probable contradiction to actuality, these are some of the complexities casting a shadow on simplistic and homogenized notions of the nation. There are nations within nations and histories within histories. In Zakir, the professor of history in Husain's *Basti*, as Muhammad Umar Memon remarks in his Introduction to *Basti*, the writer seems to explore his entire cultural identity extending back through a millennium and a half of Muslim history. As a citizen of the new nation, the consciousness of being a Pakistani has to reconcile with the history he carries from India, both at the personal as well as the collective level. In fact there has to be a juxtaposition of the personal with the collective histories of migrancy and exile. Different ideologies and politics formulate and construct the idea of the nation.

Migrancy, it is evident, also meant migrancy of ideas and histories. The new location, thus, became a site for internal and external conflict between the self and the 'other', the other as the self, the other face-to-face with the self. When Ghani the Mussalman in Mohan Rakesh's story 'Malbe Ka Malik' (His Heap of Rubble)[17] comes to India seven years after Partition to see the rubble of his house, the experience demolishes the psychologically preserved walls of his house. He has to come to terms with new realities. The professed ideology of nation state which earlier may not have had any meaning for him becomes real and we imagine he goes back to a Pakistan that is a freshly defined Pakistan. India translates itself as the other. There are obviously territorial imperatives of the security of the self at work.

The story of Partition and India, we are aware, will be far from even half told if we do not pay attention to the plight of the innumerable women, mauled, raped and abused in every way in the mayhem of Partition. In Rajinder Singh Bedi's Urdu story 'Lajwanti', the girl who is Lajjo to her husband before Partition becomes for him the deified Lajwanti (touch-me-not) after she has been through the gruesome experience of male assault during Partition. The husband can have reverence for her but not love and passion. He can respect her and deify her but cannot bring himself to have a normal relationship with a 'dishonoured' wife. The loss of honour of the woman transforms it all. Lines from Amrita Pritam's Punjabi poem 'Aj Akhan Waris Sah Nun' indicate the crucial and touching difference between the pre- and the post-partition scenario *vis-à-vis* the female consciousness in a male-dominant world: the woman's self gets translated as the other to herself as well as another:

> Today I implore Waris Shah
> to speak up from his grave
> and turn over a page of
> the Book of Love
> When a daughter of the fabled Punjab wept
> He gave tongue to her silent grief
> Today a million daughters weep
> But where is Waris Shah
> To give voice to their woes?[18]

It is difficult to forget the poignant scene from Bhisham Sahni's Hindi novel *Tamas* in which in a rioting town, a large group of Sikh women jump into a well one by one to save their honour. Women pile up in the well till it gets to be so full that the last few of them cannot jump into it! Women were so totally out of both, the political decisions that created the chaos as well as the horror of violence that followed them. And yet they were the worst targets of brutality from the men of both the communities. On the one hand, the Pakistani Urdu writer Farkhanda Lodi's story 'Parbati', written soon after the 1965 Indo-Pak war, presents a picture of the culturally composite identity of woman in Parbati/Parveen, suggesting that women know no frontiers: "she had forgotten that there are countries on this earth, and countries have borders and borders are guarded".[19] On the other hand, as Samina Rahman, an educationist from Pakistan, perceives, there is that mirror effect between two hostile worlds in which as each reflects and imitates the other—and in fact creates the other, humanity is abandoned.[20]

From within the existential angst of homelessness, the Partition-affected writer in India and Pakistan has constantly been deconstructing that past when India meant home, the India that has now become the other. The narrative of the present reacts, counters, readjusts with the memory of the past. The idea of the nation has developed now as a major area of academic discussion. Far from remaining confined to a simple geopolitical space, it is an entity constructed by concepts, ideologies and histories. Partition destabilized the unquestioned legitimacy of the earlier ideals, further problematizing the very idea of nation and identity.

India had now to be seen as distinct from Pakistan which in turn got set to work out its own identity. Gradually India, then, was translated as the other by all those who had carried their own India across borders and across time. Indeed the relationship between the original self and the translated other is in harmony when the primal connections are realized. But the conflict between the two emerges and sharpens in utter frustration with the surfacing of the points of departure from the perception of what was the original.

NOTES AND REFERENCES

1. Mushirul Hasan, ed., *India Partitioned: The Other Side of Freedom*, Introduction (New Delhi: Roli Books, 1995, 1997), 10.

2. Intezar Husain, *Basti*, Trans. Frances W. Pritchett (New Delhi: Indus, HarperCollins Publishers India, 1995).
3. Intezar Husain, *Basti*, 83.
4. Rahi Masoom Raza, *Adha Gaon*, translated into English as *The Feuding Families of Village Gangauli* by Gillian Wright (Delhi: Penguin Books, 1994).
5. This expression is used by Mushirul Hasan in the Introduction to *India Partitioned*.
6. Joginder Paul, *Khwabro*, translated into English by Sunil Trivedi and Sukrita Paul Kumar as *Sleepwalkers* (Delhi: Katha, 1998).
7. Joginder Paul, *Khwabro*, translated into English by Sunil Trivedi and Sukrita Paul Kumar, *Sleepwalkers*, 12.
8. Intezar Husain, *Basti*, 142.
9. Joginder Paul, *Khwabro*, translated into English by Sunil Trivedi and Sukrita Paul Kumar, *Sleepwalkers*, 46.
10. Intezar Husain, *Basti*, 149.
11. Intezar Husain, *Basti*, 148.
12. Intezar Husain, *Basti*, 167.
13. Kamleshwar, *Laute Hue Musafir* (Allahabad: Lokbharti Prakashan), 61.
14. Kamleshwar, *Laute Hue Musafir*, 254.
15. Intezar Husain, *Basti*, 263.
16. Ali Imam Naqvi, 'The Vultures of the Parsi Cemetery', in Mushirul Hasan (ed.), *India Partitioned: The Other Side of Freedom* (New Delhi: Roli Books, 1995, 1997), 295.
17. Mohan Rakesh, *Malbe ka Malik*, translated into English as *His Heap of Rubble* by Harish Trivedi, in Sukrita Paul Kumar (ed.), *Breakthrough* (Shimla: IIAS, 1993).
18. Amrita Pritam, *Aj Akhan Waris Sah Nun*, translated by N.S. Tasneem and edited by K.M. George, *Modern Indian Literature* (New Delhi: Sahitya Akademi).
19. Farkhandha Lodi, 'Parbati', translated and edited by Samina Rehman, *In Her Own Time* (Lahore: ASR Publications, 1994), 71.
20. Samina Rehman, *In her Own Time*, Introduction (Lahore: ASR Publications, 1994).

11

Ensuring Harmony in a Pluralistic Society—Role of Government

D.R. Kaarthikeyan

The purpose of this forum for cross-cultural conversation is—as has been stated—to promote a sense of human solidarity and to discern ways and means for removing various sorts of asymmetries and polarities that create the dominant and marginalized groups within national and international contexts while recognizing the legitimacy of race and religion, nationality, ethnicity, gender and other criteria for construing our identities.

We have come together to express our views on various aspects of this very vital and interesting theme, which is most relevant in the contemporary fractured world. The main aim of my deliberation is to focus on the role that India can play today in the plural and often strife-stricken national as well as international scenes and how the existing imbalances can be rectified by reimagining India.

I would like to begin by quoting from PTI report from Washington on 25 December 2010 from the WikiLeaks. It says, as below:

India's pluralistic society exemplary
December 25, 2010 6:28:30 PM | PTI | Washington

At a time when nations around the globe are losing ground to extremism, India's tradition of tolerance and its management of a large and diverse society can be an important learning ground for the world. Indeed, a US cable from its New Delhi embassy said in 2006 that in the democratic, multi-religious and multi-ethnic society that India is, secularism is synonymous to tolerance of all faiths and extremists are far outnumbered by 'secular' moderates. It has been also mentioned there that "India's large Muslim population, and that community's relatively positive relations with its Hindu majority, also offer insights on how we can more effectively engage in the battle of ideas against violent extremism within a democratic, pluralistic society".

One reads further: "We can learn a great deal from India's management of its large society to minimise extremist ideologies. India enjoys a democratic, multi-religious, multi-cultural, heterogeneous, multi-ethnic society where all major world religions are practised freely."

"Isolated elements of religious extremism of many varieties have, however, occurred in India—notably among Hindus, Muslims, and Sikhs—although extremists as a whole are by far outnumbered by 'secular' moderates", the US embassy said, praising the secular democratic tradition of India.

The US accuses WikiLeaks of stealing its secret cables, though it has refused to either deny or confirm their authenticity.

It said in the Indian context, secularism stands for tolerance for all faiths and does not imply life devoid of religion, although religious freedom—including atheism—is protected and guaranteed by the Constitution and a long history of court precedent.

"At a time when many nations appear to be losing ground to extremist movements, India's trendlines are pointing in the right direction, bolstered by strong indigenous traditions of communal co-habitation, non-violent political protest, a free press", the embassy cable said.

It also noted a realization by politicians that religious hatred is not a vote getter among the "increasingly savvy, globalised, and prosperous Indian electorate".

However, it said a risk of isolated outbreaks of sectarian violence remains.

"… Especially in response to the terrorism that has plagued India for decades, or when provoked by regional politicians for their narrow political purposes (for example, the recently passed anti-conversion legislation in Rajasthan)", the cable said.

The embassy noted that a special public diplomacy effort is being made to engage with Indian Muslims, including young students and other young people, and to foster interfaith dialogue among India's multicultural and multi-religious communities.

"Our outreach ranges from one-on-one engagement with elites to press interviews to mass-audience interaction to overcome misperceptions and stereotypes. We also monitor and report trends in religious extremism", it said.

The above is the assessment of American diplomats in Delhi that secularism and tolerance still reign supreme in India.

Speaking of 'ensuring harmony in a pluralistic society', the question that arises at first is, what can be described as a pluralistic society?

This is any society in which citizens can legally and publicly hold multiple competing religious views and are allowed to choose for themselves what religious beliefs, if any, they wish to hold.

The condition of being multiple or plural means:

(1)   A condition in which numerous distinct ethnic, religious or cultural groups are present and tolerated within a society.

(2)   The belief that such a condition is desirable or socially beneficial.

Indian family law is complex, with each religion having its own specific laws which they adhere to. In most states, registering of marriages and divorces is not compulsory. There are separate laws governing Hindus, Muslims, Christians, Sikhs and followers of other religions. The exception to this rule is in the state of Goa, where a Portuguese uniform civil code is in place, in which all religions have a common law regarding marriages, divorces and adoption.

Freedom of religion in India is a fundamental right guaranteed by the country's Constitution. Freedom of religion is established in tradition as Hinduism does not recognize labels of exclusive claims of any distinct religions and has no concept of blasphemy. Every citizen of India has a right to practice and promote their religion peacefully. This is not to say that there have not been many incidents of religious intolerance which have resulted in riots and pogroms. However, these incidents have been condemned by the governmental administrations, private businesses and judicial systems.

India is one of the most diverse nations in terms of religion. Even though Hindus form close to 80 per cent of the population, the Indian Muslims form the third largest Muslim population in the world, and the country also has large Sikh, Christian and Zoroastrian populations. It is home to the holiest shrines of four world religions: Hinduism, Buddhism, Jainism and Sikhism.

Modern India came into existence in 1947 as a secular nation and the Indian Constitution's preamble states that India is a secular state. It is noteworthy that India has had a Hindu President (Pratibha Patil), Muslim Vice President (M. Hamid Ansari), a Sikh Prime Minister (Manmohan Singh) and an atheist (Christian by birth) Defence Minister, A.K. Antony. The leader of the largest party, the Indian National Congress, Sonia Gandhi is a Christian, while the leader of the opposition is Sushma Swaraj, a Hindu. India's ex-President A.P.J. Abdul Kalam was a Muslim. Out of the 12 Presidents of India since Independence, three have been Muslims. India had a prominent former Defence Minister (George Fernandes), a Christian (though not practicing) and a Hindu minister controlling foreign affairs. India's ex-Air Force Chief, Fali H. Major, was a Parsi.

REFUGE FROM RELIGIOUS PERSECUTION

India, with its traditional tolerance, has served as a refuge for groups that have encountered persecution elsewhere.

- **Jews:** Jews in India were granted lands and trading rights. The oldest of the three longest established Jewish communities in India, traders from Judea and Israel arrived in the city of Cochin, in what is now Kerala, 2,500 years ago and are now known as Cochin Jews. According to recordings by Jews, the date of the first arrival is given at 562 BC. In 68 AD, more Jews fled to Kerala to escape attacks by the Romans on Jerusalem.
- **Christians:** Christianity is believed to have come to India in the first century.
- **Parsi:** The Zoroastrians from Iran arrived in India fleeing from religious persecution in their native Iran in the ninth century. They flourished in India and in eighteenth to nineteenth centuries intervened on behalf of their co-religionists still in Iran. They have

produced India's pioneering industrialist house of Tatas and one
of the only two Indian Field Marshals S.F. Manekshaw.

* **Tibetan Buddhists:** India is now home to the Dalai Lama, the
revered head of the Vajrayana Buddhism of Tibet.

Albert Einstein could not have expressed this better, when he said:
"Laws alone can't secure freedom of expression; in order that every man
presents his views without penalty, there must be spirit of tolerance in
the entire population."

We have to evolve a society that will respect differences and celebrate
differences. What are the various issues on tolerance?

(1)   Tolerance for people's opinion
(2)   Tolerance for people's culture
(3)   Tolerance for people's belief system
(4)   Tolerance for people's styles

In fact, such an attitude, be it that of an individual or a collection
of them, that is, society, is the hallmark of civilization and that is what
characterizes and differentiates life from sheer existence. Honesty
and integrity—both in thought and action, independence and
interdependence—in their wholesome and positive manifestations
would distinguish a civilized society in its true sense. It is for each
individual to strive to inculcate these eternal values in him or her, and
that alone would be the surest path and unfailing guarantee for a civilized
society and its future.

The self-image of India is reflected in the Indian Constitution. It also
provides important information and rules with regard to the rights of
minorities—religious as well as linguistic.

CONSTITUTIONAL SAFEGUARDS FOR RELIGIOUS AND LINGUISTIC MINORITIES OF INDIA

Though the Constitution of India does not define the word 'minority'
and only refers to 'minorities' and speaks of those 'based on religion

or language', the rights of the minorities have been spelt out in the Constitution in detail.

'Common Domain' and 'Separate Domain' of Rights of Minorities Provided in the Constitution

The Constitution provides two sets of rights of minorities which can be placed in 'common domain' and 'separate domain'. The rights which fall in the 'common domain' are those which are applicable to all the citizens of our country. The rights which fall in the 'separate domain' are those which are applicable to the minorities only and these are reserved to protect their identity. The distinction between 'common domain' and 'separate domain' and their combination have been well kept and protected in the Constitution. The preamble to the Constitution declares the state to be 'secular' and this is a special relevance for the religious minorities. Equally relevant for them, especially, is the declaration of the Constitution in its preamble that all citizens of India are to be secured 'liberty of thought, expression, belief, faith and worship' and 'equality of status and of opportunity'.

'Common Domain', the Directive Principles of State Policy—Part IV of the Constitution

The Constitution has made provisions for the Fundamental Rights in Part III, which the state has to comply with and these are also judicially enforceable. There is another set of non-justiciable rights stated in Part IV, which are connected with social and economic rights of the people. These rights are known as 'Directive Principles of State Policy', which legally are not binding upon the state but are "fundamental in the governance of the country and it shall be the duty of the State to apply these principles in making laws" (Article 37). Part IV of the Constitution of India, containing non-justiciable Directive Principles of State Policy, includes the following provisions having significant implications for the minorities:

> (1) Obligation of the state 'to endeavour to eliminate inequalities in status, facilities and opportunities' amongst individuals

and groups of people residing in different areas or engaged in different vocations (Article 38 [2])

(2) Obligation of state 'to promote with special care' the educational and economic interests of 'the weaker sections of the people' (besides scheduled castes and scheduled tribes) (Article 46)

'Common Domain', the Fundamental Duties—Part IV A of the Constitution

Part IV A of the Constitution, relating to Fundamental Duties as provided in Article 51 A applies in full to all citizens, including those belonging to minorities. Article 51 A which is of special relevance for the minorities stipulates as following:

(1) Citizens' duty to promote harmony and the spirit of common brotherhood amongst all the people of India 'transcending religious, linguistic and regional or sectional diversities'

(2) Citizens' duty to value and preserve the rich heritage of our composite culture'

'Common Domain', the Fundamental Rights—Part III of the Constitution

The Constitution has provided a definite space for both the 'domains', that is, 'common' as well as 'separate'. In Part III of the Constitution, which deals with the Fundamental Rights, is divided into two parts, namely, (a) the rights which fall in the 'common domain' and (b) the rights which go to the 'separate domain'. In the 'common domain', the following Fundamental Rights and freedoms are covered:

(1) People's right to 'equality before the law' and 'equal protection of the laws' (Article 14)

(2) Prohibition of discrimination against citizens on grounds of religion, race, caste, sex or place of birth (Article 15 [1] and [2])

(3) Authority of state to make 'any special provision for the advancement of any socially and educationally backward classes

of citizens' (besides the scheduled castes and scheduled tribes) (Article 15 [4])

(4) Citizens' right to 'equality of opportunity' in matters relating to employment or appointment to any office under the state—and prohibition in this regard of discrimination on grounds of religion, race, caste, sex or place of birth (Article 16 [1] and [2])

(5) Authority of state to make 'any provision for the reservation of appointments or posts in favour of any backward class of citizens which, in the opinion of the State, is not adequately represented in the services under the State' (Article 16[4])

(6) People's freedom of conscience and right to freely profess, practice and propagate religion—subject to public order, morality and other Fundamental Rights (Article 25[1])

(7) Right of 'every religious denomination or any section thereof—subject to public order, morality and health—to establish and maintain institutions for religious and charitable purposes', 'manage its own affairs in matters of religion' and own and acquire movable immovable property and administer it 'in accordance with law' (Article 26)

(8) Prohibition against 'compelling any person to pay taxes for promotion of any particular religion' (Article 27)

(9) People's 'freedom as to attendance at religious instruction or religious worship in educational institutions' wholly maintained, recognized or aided by the state (Article 28)

'Separate Domain' of Minority Rights

The minority rights provided in the Constitution which fall in the category of 'separate domain' are as under:

(1) Right of 'any section of the citizens' to 'conserve' its 'distinct language, script or culture' (Article 29[1])

(2) Restriction on denial of admission to any citizen to any educational institution maintained or aided by the state 'on grounds only of religion, race, caste, language or any of them' (Article 29[2])

(3) Right of all religious and linguistic minorities to establish and administer educational institutions of their choice (Article 30[1])

(4) Freedom of minority-managed educational institutions from discrimination in the matter of receiving aid from the state (Article 30[2])

(5) Special provision relating to the language spoken by a section of the population of any state (Article 347)

(6) Provision for facilities for instruction in mother tongue at primary stage (Article 350 A)

(7) Provision for a special officer for linguistic minorities and his duties (Article 350 B)

(8) Sikh community's right of 'wearing and carrying of kirpans' (Explanation 1 below Article 25)

INDIA'S MULTICULTURALISM INTERWOVEN IN THE CONSTITUTION

The various articles of the Constitution providing rights to the minorities clearly and firmly point out to only one direction: that of a multi-religious, multicultural, multilingual and multi-racial Indian society, interwoven into an innate unity by the common thread of national integration and communal harmony. By the yardstick adopted by the framers of the Constitution and crystallized into its provisions, the Indian nation is not just a conglomeration of individual inhabitants of this state; it comprises of two distinct categories of constituents. The two-tier commonwealth of Indian nation includes, on one hand, every citizen of India individually and, on the other hand, the multitude of religious, linguistic, cultural and ethnic groups among its citizens. The Indian nation is an enormous coparcenary in which the individual citizens are also members of their own respective branches taking the form of religious, cultural, linguistic and ethnic groups. And all these groups, like all individuals, have the same Fundamental Rights to enjoy and the same Fundamental Duties to discharge.

PROTECTION OF WEAKER SECTIONS IN INDIAN PLURALISTIC SOCIETY

The social pluralism of India, as fortified by the unique constitutional concept of secularism, raises the need for the protection and development of all sorts of weaker sections of the Indian citizenry—whether this 'weakness' is based on numbers or on social, economic or educational status of any particular group. The Constitution, therefore, speaks of religious and linguistic minorities, scheduled castes, scheduled tribes and backward classes and makes—or leaves room for making—for them special provisions of various nature and varying import.

The National Commission for Minorities (NCM) is a body constituted by the Government of India to monitor and evaluate the progress of people classified as minorities by the Indian government. Essentially the minorities in India consist of followers of all religions other than Hinduism and weaker sections in the Hindu community. The commission is also referred to as the Minority Commission. It was formed as a result of an act of the Indian Parliament in 1993.

National Commission for Minorities (Amendment) Act 1995

Functions of the commission:

The commission shall perform all or any of the following functions, namely:

(1) Evaluate the progress of the development of minorities under the union and states.

(2) Monitor the working of the safeguards provided in the Constitution and in laws enacted by Parliament and the state legislatures.

(3) Make recommendations for the effective implementation of safeguards for the protection of the interests of minorities by the central government or the state governments.

(4) Look into specific complaints regarding deprivation of rights and safeguards of the minorities and take up such matters with the appropriate authorities.

(5) Cause studies to be undertaken into problems arising out of any discrimination against minorities and recommend measures for their removal.

(6) Conduct studies, research and analysis on the issues relating to socio-economic and educational development of minorities.

(7) Suggest appropriate measures in respect of any minority to be undertaken by the central government or the state governments.

(8) Make periodical or special reports to the central government on any matter pertaining to minorities and in particular the difficulties confronted by them.

(9) Any other matter which may be referred to it by the central government.

Right to Freedom of Religion

Article 25 of the Constitution guarantees:

Freedom of conscience and free profession, practice and propagation of religion.

(1) Subject to public order, morality and health and to the other provisions of this part, all persons are equally entitled to freedom of conscience and the right freely to profess, practise and propagate religion.

(2) Nothing in this article shall affect the operation of any existing law or prevent the state from making any law:

   a. regulating or restricting any economic, financial, political or other secular activity which may be associated with religious practice; and

   b. providing for social welfare and reform or the throwing open of Hindu religious institutions of a public character to all classes and sections of Hindus.

Explanation I: The wearing and carrying of kirpans shall be deemed to be included in the profession of the Sikh religion.

Explanation II: In sub-clause (b) of clause (2), the reference to Hindus shall be construed as including a reference to persons professing the Sikh, Jaina or Buddhist religion, and the reference to Hindu religious institutions shall be construed accordingly.

Article 26 Guarantees Freedom to Manage Religious Affairs

Subject to public order, morality and health, every religious denomination or any section thereof shall have the right:

(1) to establish and maintain institutions for religious and charitable purposes;
(2) to manage its own affairs in matters of religion;
(3) to own and acquire movable and immovable property; and
(4) to administer such property in accordance with law.

Article 27. Freedom as to Payment of Taxes for Promotion of any Particular Religion

No person shall be compelled to pay any taxes, the proceeds of which are specifically appropriated in payment of expenses for the promotion or maintenance of any particular religion or religious denomination.

Cultural and Educational Rights

Article 29. Protection of interests of minorities:

(1) Any section of the citizens residing in the territory of India or any part thereof having a distinct language, script or culture of its own shall have the right to conserve the same.
(2) No citizen shall be denied admission into any educational institution maintained by the state or receiving aid out of state funds on grounds only of religion, race, caste, language or any of them.

Article 51A (e), Fundamental Duties: It shall be the duty of every citizens of India:

(*1*) to promote harmony and the spirit of common brotherhood amongst all the people of India transcending religious, linguistic and regional or sectional diversities; to renounce practices derogatory to the dignity of women; and

(*2*) to value and preserve the rich heritage of our composite culture.

Indian Penal Code 153 A Punishes Instigation of Religious Disharmony

153A.1 (Promoting enmity between different groups on ground of religion, race, place of birth, residence, language, etc., and doing acts prejudicial to maintenance of harmony.)

(*1*) Whoever:
- (a) by words, either spoken or written, or by signs or by visible representations or otherwise, promotes or attempts to promote, on grounds of religion, race, place of birth, residence, language, caste or community or any other ground whatsoever, disharmony or feelings of enmity, hatred or ill-will between different religious, racial, language or regional groups or castes or communities; or
- (b) commits any act which is prejudicial to the maintenance of harmony between different religious, racial, language or regional groups or castes or communities, and which disturbs or is likely to disturb the public tranquillity; or
- (c) organizes any exercise, movement, drill or other similar activity intending that the participants in such activity shall use or be trained to use criminal force or violence or knowing it to be likely that the participants in such activity will use or be trained to use criminal force or violence, or participates in such activity intending to use or be trained to use criminal force or violence or knowing it to be likely that the participants in such activity will use or be trained to use criminal force or violence, against any religious,

racial, language or regional group or caste or community and such activity for any reason whatsoever causes or is likely to cause fear or alarm or a feeling of insecurity amongst members of such religious, racial, language or regional group or caste or community, shall be punished with imprisonment which may extend to three years, or with fine, or with both.

(2) Offence committed in place of worship, etc.: Whoever commits an offence specified in subsection (1) in any place of worship or in any assembly engaged in the performance of religious worship or religious ceremonies shall be punished with imprisonment which may extend to five years and shall also be liable to fine.

Indian Penal Code 295

295. Injuring or defiling place of worship, with intent to insult the religion of any class.

Whoever destroys, damages or defiles any place of worship, or any object held sacred by any class of persons with the intention of thereby insulting the religion of any class of persons or with the knowledge that any class of persons is likely to consider such destruction, damage or defilement as an insult to their religion, shall be punished with imprisonment of either description for a term which may extend to two years, or with fine, or with both.

Indian Penal Code—295A

Section 295A. Deliberate and malicious acts, intended to outrage religious feelings or any class by insulting its religion or religious beliefs.

Whoever, with deliberate and malicious intention of outraging the religious feelings of any class of 2 (citizens of India), 3 (by words, either spoken or written, or by signs or by visible representations or otherwise), insults or attempts to insult the religion or the religious beliefs of that class, shall be punished with imprisonment of either description for a term which may extend to 4 (three years' imprisonment), or with fine, or with both.

IPC 296. Disturbing Religious Assembly

Whoever voluntarily causes disturbance to any assembly lawfully engaged in the performance of religious worship, or religious ceremonies, shall be punished with imprisonment of either description for a term which may extend to one year, or with fine, or with both.

IPC 297. Trespassing on Burial Places, Etc.

Whoever with the intention of wounding the feelings of any person or of insulting the religion of any person or with the knowledge that the feelings of any person are likely to be wounded or that the religion of any person is likely to be insulted, thereby commits any trespass in any place of worship or on any place of sepulture or any place set apart for the performance of funeral rites or as a depository for the remains of the dead or offers any indignity .o any human corpse or causes disturbance to any persons assembled for the performance of funeral ceremonies.

IPC 298. Uttering Words, Etc., with Deliberate Intent to Wound Religious Feelings

Whoever with the deliberate intention of wounding the religious feelings of any person, utters any word or makes any sound in the hearing of that person or makes any gesture in the sight of that person or places any object in the sight of that person shall be punished with imprisonment of either description for a term which may extend to one year, or with fine, or with both.

PRIMARY ROLE OF GOVERNMENT IN ENSURING RELIGIOUS HARMONY IN INDIA

India has been home to several traditions, religions, languages, cultures, caste and creed since thousands of years. There has been enormous diversity of all kinds. Apart from the traditions and religions that are home grown, practically almost all major religions of the world came to India from time to time and received wide acceptance.

The perennial philosophy of ancient India since thousands of years has been expressed in such famous statements as *ekam sat vipra bahudha vadanti* (reality is one, the wise call it by many names); *vasudhaiva kutumbakam* (the entire world is one family); *sarva dharma samabhav* (equal respect for all religions). The prayer has always been: may everyone in this world be happy, may everyone be free from disease, may everyone see prosperity, may none come to grief.

While the maintenance of law and order and enforcement of the above provisions of the Constitution and specific penal provisions are the responsibility of the various state/provincial/local governments through their own police and magisterial machinery, the national, federal Government of India has an overall responsibility of maintaining and encouraging harmony between various religious groups by ensuring compliance with the provisions of the Constitution and various enactments mentioned above through its own police, investigative and enforcement machinery.

12

Negotiating Compromises in Cross-cultural Conversations

Dietmar Rothermund

AGAINST DETERMINISM AND ESSENTIALISM

The human mind favours convincing causal explanations of the course of history and of the coherence of society. This implies a preference for determinism and essentialism as embodied in the ideology of historical materialism and in the holistic concept of culture which encompasses all aspects of social life. Cross-cultural conversation is incompatible with these tendencies. The Marxist doctrine according to which material conditions determine human consciousness precludes meaningful exchanges of ideas between those whose material conditions are different. Similarly, the essentialist idea according to which each culture constitutes a seamless texture of unique social relations negates the possibility of meaningful communication between different cultures which coexist as isolated monads. In recent decades, great efforts have been made to escape from the trap of social determinism and of cultural essentialism. These efforts concentrate on claiming the autonomy of the individual whose decisions are supposed to be the only relevant base of social life. In the social sciences, this approach has been termed 'methodological individualism'. The most radical representation of this individualism is embodied in the Rational Choice Theory, which postulates that human beings only act rationally if they aim at maximizing their self-interest. If one can define this interest, one can arrive at a kind of calculus of decision-making which would make individual behaviour predictable. Determinism and essentialism in this way re-enter the interpretation of human behaviour through the back door. Amartya Sen has criticized Rational Choice Theory and has pointed out that it "reflects an extremely limited understanding of reason and rationality".[1] Instead, he recommends a broadly conceived theory of social choice, which takes account of the world around the decision-making individual and of the various different interests which he/she may have. One of these interests could be 'agency freedom', which may not at all coincide with a more narrowly conceived 'self-interest'. Sen mentions the example of Mahatma Gandhi to illustrate this point.[2] 'Agency' has become a key term in the discourse of those who have turned against determinism and essentialism in order to emphasize the freedom of the individual from social forces which totally control him or her.

AGENCY FREEDOM AND THE NEED FOR NEGOTIATION

The emphasis on 'agency' led to a new concept of culture which was no longer seen as an all-encompassing phenomenon but rather as a resource at the disposal of the individual. According to Jürgen Habermas, this resource supplies human beings with a fund of knowledge which enables them to interpret the world in which they live.[3] The uses made of this resource depend on individual decisions whose 'agency' is not constrained by forces which subject him/her to predetermined social conditions. The reliance on 'agency' begs the question how individual autonomy should be reconciled with the interests of other individuals. The idea of a 'social contract' has been suggested so as to prevent a chaos of conflicting interests. In the West, Thomas Hobbes has been a pioneer of such 'contractualism'. But even in ancient India, this idea was well known. It was referred to as the *matsyanyaya* (the rule that the big fish swallow the small fish). In order to prevent this, men must elect a king who protects them from such chaos. When Kautilya wrote his *Arthashastra* (a treatise on politics) presumably about 300 BC, he referred to this theory, but he did not do so in order to recommend it as a golden rule of right conduct; instead, he quoted a secret agent of the king as propagating it among the people. Kautilya commented on this type of propaganda that it was good to make the people believe in this kind of theory, but he obviously did not believe in it himself.[4] He seems to have been aware of the fact that a 'social contract' is at best a regulative idea and cannot be derived from actual practice. Modern critics of 'contractualism' are not influenced by Kautilya's cynical 'realism', but they see in it a transcendental construct which obstructs human endeavour. Amartya Sen has dedicated his recent book *The Idea of Justice* to a critique of the limits of contractarianism.[5] He stresses instead the practice of social realization with regard to enhancement of justice rather than a quest for a perfectly just society.

The terms 'negotiation' and 'compromise' are conspicuous by their absence in Sen's work, but his emphasis on public reasoning and social choice indicates that he would be in sympathy with those who highlight 'negotiation' as a necessary corollary of 'agency' in the field of social theory. Probably his training as an economist has led to his avoidance of the term 'negotiation' as it has a specific meaning in economics which is quite different from that which makes it so attractive for social theorists. In fact, different disciplines which are not affected by such previous meanings of the term have adopted it with great enthusiasm. Two examples from literary history and social representations theory will show how 'negotiation' has been interpreted creatively by scholars working in those fields.

In literary history, Stephen Greenblatt's *Shakespearean Negotiations* have won great acclaim.[6] He argues that Shakespeare was involved in continuous negotiations with his environment, drawing on its social energy and widening the scope of poetic imagination. The 'agency' of the author relies on the feedback of his society and is inspired by it. Greenblatt explores authorial intentions by linking them to the social conditions of the author's times. In this context, 'negotiations' refer to the creative interaction of the author with his environment. Mahatma Gandhi also 'negotiated' in this way both with Indian and British society.

In the field of social psychology, 'negotiations' also play an important role. Social representations theory which charts the crossroads between the individual and society has adopted this term in order to explore identity formation. A study of immigrant youths in Norway provides a good example of this endeavour.[7] The authors combine two empirical studies, of which the first one traces the references to immigrants in Norwegian newspapers and their change over time while the second one reports the results of group interviews with young people who have grown up in Norway as children of immigrants and are Norwegian citizens but 'negotiate' their ethnic identities in different ways. The spectrum of their negotiations reaches from an assertation of 'belonging' to the Norwegian nation to an outright rejection of it and an emphasis on their original ethnic identity. While the first study reflects the social representations of immigrants by the host society, the second one shows how young people with an immigrant background react to these representations by defining their own position. Of course, *Shakespearean Negotiations* which cover a broad spectrum are of a different order than the more narrowly conceived quest of young immigrants for an ethnic identity. But basically all such negotiations are open deliberations which presume agency freedom as well as the need of coming to terms with a social environment. Open deliberations require a receptivity for the arguments of others and a freedom from domination which would preclude such an openness.

THE OPENNESS OF COMMUNICATIVE REASON

Philosophers of such different pedigree as Jürgen Habermas and Hans-Georg Gadamer have stressed open communication as the foundation of human interaction. In his theory of communicative reason, Habermas stresses the human ability to say 'No' to somebody else's statement.[8] Gadamer asserts the hermeneutic priority of raising questions. He explains that the openness of questions is due to the fact that the answer is not predetermined.[9] Richard Rorty's conversationalism and his recognition of a multiplicity of vocabularies call for an unconditional openness.[10] But these pleas of modern philosophers only repeat what was asserted even in very ancient times. Ram A. Mall who advocates an 'intercultural philosophy' refers to the example of the dialogue between King Menander (Milinda) and the Buddhist monk Nagasena.[11] The king wants to have a dialogue with the monk who accepts his invitation on one condition: it should proceed according to the rules of scholars and not of kings. The sage explains the difference by pointing out that scholars listen to each other's arguments and are open to compromise whereas kings take a stand and punish those who dare to contradict them. Menander then accepted Nagasena's condition and they embarked on a cross-cultural conversation without the threat of royal domination. Although Menander is not a Buddhist, he shows great interest in the fundamental principles of the Buddhist faith. He is intrigued by the Buddhist denial of an individual human soul while nevertheless believing in rebirth which is explained in terms of the renewed combination of consciousness with material elements of human existence.

The openness of cross-cultural conversations is, however, not an end in itself. It remains a mere intellectual entertainment if it does not inform human actions. Therefore, cross-cultural conversations must raise questions of ethics. Modern analytical philosophers have neglected ethics because they assumed that ethics are necessarily related to metaphysics which ought to be avoided by them. It was due to the pioneering work of John Rawls that ethics once more moved into the centre of philosophical attention.

ETHICS WITHOUT METAPHYSICS: THE QUEST FOR A COMMON DENOMINATOR OF HUMAN COMMITMENT

In the days when metaphysics reigned supreme, ethics were presumed to be derived from divine commandments. When metaphysics were rejected, a new common denominator had to be found on which ethics could be based. John Rawls found this denominator in the 'overlapping consensus' of the members of a society. He stressed that this consensus was not a mere modus vivendi which would change when power relations favouring one side or the other led to a revision of an ephemeral consensus.[12] An 'overlapping consensus' was stable because it was based on shared values. But those values must not be derived from 'comprehensive doctrines' by which Rawls meant religious or quasi-religious doctrines. An appeal to such doctrines could easily lead to a rejection of values held by those who adhered to other doctrines. This may explain why Rawls never referred to Mahatma Gandhi in his work. In his *Theory of Justice*, Rawls has devoted a whole chapter to the right of resistance. At least here one would have expected an evaluation of Gandhi's campaigns of non-violent resistance. But Gandhi is conspicuous by his absence from the discussion of the right of resistance. As it is impossible to assume that Rawls had never heard of Gandhi, avoiding him must have had a systematic reason. It seems that Rawls saw in Gandhi a religious leader attached to a 'comprehensive doctrine' who could not support an overlapping consensus. In fact, Gandhi did establish such a consensus in South Africa where both Hindus and Muslims joined his campaigns.

Rawls does not refer to 'negotiation' and 'compromise' in his work, but he comes close to the meaning of these two terms when he mentions "the virtues of tolerance and being ready to meet others halfway".[13] Meeting others halfway is not aimed at arriving at an ephemeral modus vivendi but helps to establish a social union which is of mutual benefit. Rawls quotes Wilhelm von Humboldt with approval who had stated that a social union based on the internal wants and capabilities of its members enables each to participate in the rich collective resources of all others.[14] For Rawls, the 'reasonable person' embodies the virtues which he cherishes. He writes: "Reasonable persons see that the burdens of judgment set limits to what can be reasonably justified to others, and so they endorse some form of liberty of conscience and freedom of thought."[15] In Rawls' terminology, 'reasonable' and 'rational' have different meanings. 'Reasonable' always refers to reasoning which proceeds from the assumption of a common point of departure, whereas 'rational' refers to the intrinsic rationality of thought or action. In order to demonstrate this contrast, Rawls suggests the following statement: "Their proposal was perfectly rational given their strong bargaining position, but it was nevertheless highly unreasonable, even outrageous."[16] This indicates that the reasonable person always takes the interests of others into consideration, that is, is ready to negotiate a compromise. Social cooperation is the main aim of Rawls' ethics. It is interesting to note that Herbert Spencer had made a plea for such a cooperation much earlier in his pioneering work *Social Statics*.[17] Spencer had coined the term 'survival of the fittest' before Darwin published his theory of natural selection. Later on it was assumed that the survival of the fittest referred to this type of selection and the ideology of 'social Darwinism' was based on it. Spencer, however, had coined the term in the context of his theory of social cooperation. To him, the 'fittest' were the most resourceful cooperators—or, in Rawls' terms, the most reasonable persons rather than the 'outrageous' rationalists who maximized their interests regardless of others. Spencer was a liberal thinker like Rawls but because Spencer was associated with the doctrine of evolutionism, his ideas were discarded by the later generations. This may explain why Rawls did not take note of him.

The link between individual human commitment and 'reasonable' social cooperation is very important. The challenges of our time remind us of the need to cooperate so as to solve urgent problems. Three major challenges will be singled out for a more detailed discussion.

CHALLENGES OF OUR TIME: 'THE CLASH OF CIVILIZATIONS', GLOBAL CLIMATE CHANGE, THE THREAT OF TERROR

After the collapse of the Soviet Union and the end of the Cold War, there was a need for new orientations. Unfortunately Samuel Huntington used this opportunity for his prophetic announcement of a new global conflict caused by the clash of civilizations.[18] Determinism and essentialism once more ruled supreme in his work. The civilizations were bound to clash and Huntington defined the essence of each civilization and analyzed the 'fault lines' which separated them. These 'fault lines' marked the areas of potential conflicts among those civilizations. In seismic science, fault lines are those tectonic formations in which earthquakes are frequently noticed. By adopting this metaphor, Huntington attributed a quasi-scientific character to his theory. Following Toynbee[19] who had studied the rise and fall of many civilizations, Huntington saw in them the main arenas of world history. But unlike Toynbee, Huntington was not interested in ancient civilizations; he only dealt with those which had survived until the present. He was most interested in the inevitable clash between the West (America and Europe) and the Islamic civilization. He admitted that 'agency' could not be attributed to civilizations but only to 'core states' within them. For the West, the USA was his 'core state', but he found it difficult to identify such a 'core state' for the Islamic civilization.

It seems that Huntington's theory became a self-fulfilling prophecy which greatly influenced American political leaders. They then chanced upon Iraq as the 'core state' for which Huntington had looked in vain. Actually this was the most unlikely candidate for this role. Saddam Hussain, the dictator who ruled Iraq, was a secular politician who was immensely proud of the Mesopotamian heritage of his country. He had tried to portray himself as a pious Muslim only when he was under duress and tried to appeal to Islamic solidarity. Huntington had mentioned this in his book and had not identified Iraq as the Islamic 'core state'. But the general thrust of Huntington's theory fitted in well with the intentions of American leaders.

The publication of Huntington's book was followed by an intense criticism of his views by many scholars and politicians. Among these critics was the Iranian President Mohammed Khatami who called for a 'Dialogue among Civilizations' so as to counteract Huntington's dire predictions. In a remarkable speech at the United Nations in September 2000, Khatami communicated his ideas to the world.[20] He highlighted the capacity of the Iranian civilization to integrate the methods and achievements of various cultures. He praised the contribution which Islam had made to this civilization and mentioned mysticism which provides a graceful, profound and universal language for dialogue. Finally he urged all governments to support the dialogue among civilizations.

Khatami's initiative elicited many responses. The United Nations dedicated the year 2001 to the dialogue among civilizations and many governments participated in this dialogue in their own way. In July 2003, the Government of India and United Nations Educational, Scientific and Cultural Organization (UNESCO) held a joint meeting in New Delhi dedicated to the dialogue among civilizations. It was attended by many national delegations and some specially invited scholars. However, the proceedings mainly consisted of formal statements of those delegations. They all endorsed the demand for such a dialogue, there were no objections to it, of course, but not much of substance was contributed by the delegates. However, the Iranian representative, Professor Ahmad Jalali, made an impressive speech in which he referred to Gadamer and other leading philosophers. His liberal views were surprising. As a friend of Khatami, he could express such views with impunity. His contribution was one of the few highlights of this meeting which was otherwise only a huge diplomatic affair. The tragic events of 11 September 2001 in New York and the American intervention in Iraq in March 2003 cast a shadow over this meeting. Asking for a dialogue among civilizations appeared to be like whistling in the dark in this context. Subsequent events of this type attracted less attention. The dialogue of civilizations has faded away. It is high time that it should be revived.

The other great challenge which has attracted growing attention in recent years is the global climate change and the efforts to prevent it. For a long time, mankind could take its natural environment for granted. The forces of nature were much more powerful than man and nobody could conceive of the idea that humans could do permanent and irreversible damage to this environment. The traces of this damage are to a large extent not immediately visible. The deterioration of the environment progresses like a slow disease. It is therefore very difficult to mobilize people to take action in this matter. Cross-cultural conversations are needed to bridge the gap which arises due to the perceived interests of different countries. Currently China and India urge the industrial countries of the West to do more in this field because they have historically contributed much more to the deterioration of the global environment than those countries which still have to catch up in the race towards industrialization. This is true and the current levels at which energy is consumed by industrial countries of the West as compared to the rest of the world are much too high.[21] However, references to historical guilt and the current balance of consumption may be irrelevant when climate change starts to affect those countries which plead for more leeway in this respect. For instance, if the seasonal pattern of the monsoon on which India depends is disturbed by global climate change, it will not help India if it only points to others and does not change its own course. An appeal to global solidarity in this field is certainly justified. Negotiating compromises which help to reduce global warming is of great importance. The recent summit at Cancun, Mexico, seems to have marked some progress in this direction.

Whereas there is hope that reasonable persons may find ways and means to confront the environmental challenge, there is hardly any hope with regard to the threat of terror. Terrorists are not reasonable persons, they are committed to destruction, even self-destruction. They rely on a 'comprehensive doctrine' which justifies holy war (jihad). This is an 'uncompromising' doctrine. Many Islamic theologians do not endorse this particular doctrine and would participate in cross-cultural conversations. Khatami is a prominent example of those who actively promote the idea of such conversations. The terrorists who are committed to jihad as they understand it are beyond the reach of such conversations. But they depend on an environment which nurtures them. It may be possible to influence that environment and to isolate the terrorists and close their channels of recruitment.

Germany faced a similar threat in the 1970s. Young people who were motivated by a militant ideology felt that they could destroy the capitalist system by assassinating its most prominent representatives. New terrorists were recruited again and again and quite a few people lost their lives. The method of assassinating prominent men soon proved to be futile. The victims were soon replaced by others who could do the respective jobs equally well. The 'system' could not be vanquished. A vague sympathy for the terrorists among citizens dissatisfied with the politics of those days disappeared and the recruitment of new volunteers stopped. The political climate which had nurtured the rise of terrorism had changed. The frustrations which prevail in the Islamic countries will not disappear so soon. Moreover, the terrorist movement in those countries is transnational and thus not confined to one nation as the German terrorist movement was. The frustrations in Islamic countries are caused by a perceived hostility of the West. Western attitudes hurt the self-respect of the citizens of Islamic countries. As Rawls has pointed out, "Self-respect is rooted in our self-confidence as a fully cooperating member of a society" and he adds that "without self-respect nothing may be worth doing".[22] This latter assertion indicates why the lack of self-respect leads to frustration. It seems that cross-cultural conversation is eminently suited to the enhancement of self-respect and the overcoming of frustration. Participants in such a conversation respect each other because otherwise they would not join such a conversation.

While terrorists are not amenable to reasonable arguments and would not enter into cross-cultural conversations, it could be possible that the environment in which they flourish could be influenced by a spread of self-respect among the citizens of Islamic countries. Cross-cultural conversation would provide an atmosphere for this kind of political and social change.

CROSS-CULTURAL CONVERSATION AND INTERNATIONAL MEDIATION

There is an important link between the idea of cross-cultural conversation and the method of international mediation as practised by Johan Galtung.[23] 'Negotiating compromises' is at the very heart of Galtung's endeavour. The mediator must have a deep empathy for both parties with which he has to deal. If they belong to different cultures, he must understand the respective cultural resources so as to be able to draw upon them when he talks to their representatives. Galtung recommends that the mediator must first talk to each of the parties separately in order to find out what they really want. Only after such an exploration he will bring the two parties together. They will then try to find a solution of the problem at stake. The task of the mediator is different from that of an interlocutor who is appointed by one of the parties and negotiates with the other. This other party will regard the interlocutor as somebody who argues in the interest of those who have sent him. Moreover, there is the problem of the powers of the interlocutor. Is he a plenipotentiary who can make binding decisions or is he just sent for flying kites so as to explore the intentions of the adversary? Unlike the interlocutor, the mediator is appointed by both parties jointly because they trust his impartiality. They respect his judgement and are convinced that he does not have a 'hidden agenda' of his own. He is not a plenipotentiary; the solutions found in the course of the mediation must be implemented by the parties concerned. The cross-cultural conversation which supports such attempts at mediation must be based on the foundation of a sustained intra-cultural conversation. It is often taken for granted that the 'agents' of each party concerned are thoroughly conversant with the aims and ideas of the society to which they belong. But this is not necessarily true. They may represent only a small elite or a group with a 'hidden agenda' of their own. Therefore, the meditator must be familiar with the level of the intra-cultural conversation prevailing in the society whose representatives he meets. The 'agents' may not necessarily intend to deceive him, but their consciousness of what they stand for may be limited by their own experience. There may be instances where the mediator actually has to remind those whom he is talking to of aspects of their intra-cultural conversation, of which they do not seem to be aware. This requires deep knowledge on his part and a tactful approach because he must not give the impression that he is in the possession of superior wisdom. Cross-cultural conversation can profit a great deal from the art of mediation.

THE FUTURE OF CROSS-CULTURAL CONVERSATIONS

The promotion of future cross-cultural conversations could very well begin where Khatami's initiative of a dialogue among civilizations had ended due to the vicissitudes of recent political events. The ideas of Amartya Sen and John Rawls would help to give a new thrust to this initiative. The emphasis on agency freedom and on the need for negotiating compromises would be central to it. Everybody who is assured of his agency freedom and participates in negotiating compromises enhances his self-respect in this way. This self-respect is the foundation of social cooperation.

The strategy of cross-cultural conversation should be adopted at several levels. There should be meetings of citizens of various experiences as well as get-togethers of young people. Most of these meetings may not encompass many different civilizations. In fact, huge diplomatic encounters as the one in Delhi in July 2003, which has been mentioned above, contribute very little to genuine conversations. Addressing specific themes may provide a focus to cross-cultural conversations. The training of organizers of such meetings may be a special task of those who have convened similar meetings earlier. Measures enhancing the self-confidence and self-respect of all participants should be carefully adopted. A knowledge of social psychology would be helpful in this matter. The participants should emerge from such conversations as ambassadors of cross-cultural understanding. They may also become successful mediators in a world troubled by innumerable conflicts.

NOTES AND REFERENCES

1. Amartya Sen, *The Idea of Justice* (London: Penguin Books, 2010) 180.
2. Amartya Sen, *The Idea of Justice*, 289 f.
3. Jürgen Habermas, *Theorie des kommunikativen Handelns*, Vol. 2 (Frankfurt: Suhrkamp, 1982), 209.
4. R.P. Kangle, *The Kautilya Arthasastra*, Part II (Bombay: University of Bombay, 1963), 31 f.
5. Amartya Sen, *Idea of Justice*, 126 f.
6. Stephen Greenblatt, *Shakespearean Negotiations: The Circulation of Social Energy in Renaissance England* (Berkeley: University of California Press, 1988).
7. Joshua M. Phelps and Marjan Nadim, 'Ideology and Agency in Ethnic Identity Negotiations of Immigrant Youth', *Papers ond Social Representations*, 19 (2010): 13.1–13.27.
8. Habermas, *Theorie der kommunikativen Vernunft*, Vol. 2, 114 f.
9. Hans-Georg Gadamer, *Wahrheit und Methode* (Tübingen: Mohr, 1960, 4th ed. 1975), 345.
10. Richard Rorty, *Contingency, Irony and Solidarity* (Cambridge: Cambridge University Press, 1989).
11. Ram A. Mall, 'Interkulturelle Philosoophie und die Historiographie', in Manfred Brocker/Heino Nau (eds), *Ethnozentrismus. Möglichkeiten und Grenzen des interkulturellen Dialogs* (Darmstadt: Primus, 1997), 75.
12. John Rawls, *Political Liberalism* (New York: Columbia University Press, 1993), 147 f.
13. John Rawls, *Political Liberalism*, 157.
14. John Rawls, *Political Liberalism*, 321.
15. John Rawls, *Political Liberalism*, 61.
16. John Rawls, *Political Liberalism*, 48.
17. Herbert Spencer, *Social Statics* (London: Chapman, 1851).
18. Samuel Huntington, *The Clash of Civilizations* (New York: Simon & Schuster, 1996).

19. Arnold Toynbee, *A Study of History* (Oxford: Oxford University Press, 1934–1961, 12 vols).
20. M. Khatami, *Address to the Round Table: Dialogue among Civilizations* (New York: United Nations, 5 September 2000).
21. James J. Winchester, 'Acknowledging Privilege as a Prerequisite for Solidarity: Reflections on the Ethics of Global Warming', in Anindita N. Balslev (ed.), *Toward Greater Human Solidarity: Options for a Plural World* (Kolkata: Dasgupta, 2005), 126–40).
22. Rawls, *Political Liberalism*, 318.
23. Johan Galtung, *50 Years: 100 Peace and Conflict Perspectives* (Versonnex: Transcend University Press, 2008).

13

India's Image through the Lens of Italian Travellers, from First Century AD to Twentieth Century*

Ugo Astuto

When Ms Balslev asked me to participate in this edition of Cross-cultural Conversation (CCC), I wondered how a foreign diplomat could actually contribute to the discussion. By definition, diplomats have to avoid being original and need to stir clear of any controversy.

I therefore concluded that the one useful thing I could do was to share with you the experience of others, not mine. As an Italian, out of natural curiosity, before being posted to India I have tried to read as many chronicles and journals of travellers as possible, with a special inclination towards travellers coming from my own country. I declare at the outset my partiality: I will talk mostly about Italian travellers, because I feel sufficiently versed in that respect. But there is a host of travellers coming from other places, which would deserve equal attention; and not just from Europe.

However, the viewpoint from Italy offers some clear advantages. First and foremost: antiquity.

I will therefore, with your permission, stretch a bit the definition of Italian and start with an author from the Roman Empire.

QUINTUS CURTIUS RUFUS

The culture of the Roman Empire itself was the result of different currents and streams, but its basic tenants were Hellenic. That is why

* Author's views are personal.

the travels of Alexander the Great to the East and its inroads into India, in 327 BC, were of such resonance also to the ears of travellers in later years, in Roman times. Actually, most of what we have today in terms of testimony of the adventure of Alexander comes not from the original Greek sources but from later compilations by Roman authors. There are many, but let me expand on one, who was probably born in Italy proper: Quintus Curtius Rufus, who wrote in the first century AD, in Latin, the *Historiae Alexandri Magni*, the History of Alexander the Great. In Book Nine we find a description of India.

What was the image of India in the Roman world in the first century AD? (For reference, this is the time of the Kushan kingdom in northern India and of the Han Dynasty in China.) The frame of mind of a Roman intellectual in the first century was remarkably modern in outlook: his approach to the world was rationalistic, based on Greek logic; hence the preoccupation with geographic exactness. Curtius Rufus gives us an idea of the huge continental expanse of India and of the magnitude of its great rivers: the Indus, with its tempestuous course and the majestic Ganges—"*Omnium ab Oriente fluvius eximius*", the most extraordinary of all rivers of the East.[1] The enormity and the distance of India is one of the recurrent features in chronicles of the time and of subsequent centuries, when Europeans venture beyond the Indus.

The second feature which often comes about is the wealth of the country. In the Roman world, luxury was lavishly displayed by the rich and envied by the poor. Curtius was a son of his time when describing India's wealth: "*Aurum flumina vehunt*", rivers contain gold, and "*Gemmas margaritasque mare litoribus infundit*", the sea gifts to the shore pearls and gems.[2] Curtius then expands on the wealth of Indian kings: "*Regum tamen luxuria, quam ipsi magnificentiam appellant, super gentia vitia*", the luxury of kings, that they call magnificence, goes beyond the excesses of all other peoples.[3] And here Curtius Rufus, in my opinion, uses India to take a dig at his own society, in Rome, where the opulence of the rich was generally regarded as having gone beyond any reasonable limit.

After enormity and opulence, the third recurrent feature is the marvel at the spiritual intensity of India, when the European traveller is faced with the extreme austerity of ascetics, hermits and wise men: "*Unum agreste et horridum genus est, quod sapientes vocant*", there are some people who live in isolation and austerity and they are called wise men.[4]

The so-called gymnosophists of India, a name which means naked philosophers (I assume it can be translated simply as sadhus), gained wide fame and respect in the Graeco-Roman world for their sober philosophy. The best-known anecdote about their meeting with Alexander is related not by Curtius but by another author, a Roman citizen of Greek mother tongue, born in today's Turkey: Lucius Flavius Arrianus, who wrote a history of Alexander, probably a good 60 years after Curtius.

Arrianus narrates how Alexander met the gymnosophists and how they taught him a lesson of moral philosophy:

> Every man only owns a parcel of land equal to his shadow and you, King, being a man like the others, except for your insatiable ambition and pride, you have travelled such a long and perilous way, suffering and causing mischief, only to find that very soon you will be master only of such a small parcel of land as the one sufficient for your ashes to be buried into.[5]

Arrianus took a keen interest in India; he actually wrote a book entirely devoted to India (*Indica*), most of it lost. He was also a disciple of Epictetus, probably the most admired philosopher in Rome in the second century AD. Epictetus was a Stoic whose influence over the Roman elite cannot be overstated (he personally met Emperor Hadrian). This is worth recalling, since the basic formula of Epictetus' Stoic philosophy was 'Endure and Renounce', which to my ears (and certainly to Arrianus' ears) sounded remarkably compatible with the Indian ascetics' life. We have here one of those instances where cultural roads cross and an intermingling of ideas takes place. How far and how deep? Difficult to tell.

We have already gathered through Curtius and Arrianus quite a collection of images of India from a Roman eye: immensity, wealth, wisdom. To these three, let us add a fourth feature: magick! Like most of his contemporaries, Curtius had a weak spot for astrology: he thought that some truth could definitely be found in it. That is why he relates with interest that, in India, "*Illi qui in urbibus publicis moribus degunt, siderum motu scite spectare dicuntur et future praedicere*", those who live and rule in towns, know how to read the position of the stars and can predict the future.[6] This is something Europeans have often been looking for in India: the extraordinary, the occult, the supernatural.

At the time of Curtius, the official religion of the Roman Empire was Graeco-Roman paganism. It was a remarkably open religion, with little or no dogma, that would transform and absorb most foreign cults. Roman authors believed that they could recognize their gods under disguise also in foreign religions. This is also true for India. Dionysus was associated with India, based on myths and legends current in the classical world; Roman eyes would thus duly recognize Dionysus in most local Indian cults. One can denounce such quest as a form of cultural imperialism; but in fact it helped in ensuring respect for all religions, as avatars of the one and the same message. In Rome one would find a temple devoted to "*Deus ignotus*", the unknown god, as a recognition of the fact that religious revelation takes different faces at different latitudes, but all of them are sacred.

It is now time to move on from Rome. The intense trade of goods and ideas which occurred between the Mediterranean and India in the first and second centuries AD came to a halt with the fall of the Roman Empire in the fourth century. Roman merchants and travellers were then replaced for a time by Arab traders, especially in the South.

For a time, very little direct testimony would come from European travellers to the East. As it often happens, experience was replaced with imagination. In the early Middle Ages, the recollection of the travels of Alexander the Great was transformed into an anthology of fantastic tales. There were many and different versions, consolidated around the twelfth century by the Norman poet Alexander of Bernay, under the title *Li romans d'Alixandre*, Alexander's Romance, one of the first poem written in French. The fourth book describes the exploits of Alexander in India. An India, however, which has lost all touch with reality, to become a fabulous distant world, probably not far from the Garden of Eden. The influence of such literature over later generations of Europeans should not be understated. We might see here the seeds of orientalism, in a somewhat broader sense than what Edward Said meant, but still the relegation of the Orient into 'other than' the Occident.

But to counter this trend, you could count on the solid common sense and empirical curiosity of merchants. Trade flow between Italy and India never entirely stopped; in the Middle Ages, trade with the East was the special preserve of Venice, which mastered the secrets of the Silk Road between Europe and China.

MARCO POLO

I am sure you are all familiar with the name of Marco Polo. He is only one of many Venetians who followed the route to the Orient; but he took the pain to leave us a testament of his experience, a book called *Il Milione* in Italian. He left Venice with his brothers, all of them merchants, in 1269, when he was 17 years old, and got back to Venice in 1294, after travelling on the land route over the Himalayas on his way to China and sailing back home, visiting in the process the south of India. Once in Europe, he was back to the familiar European pattern of internecine war: he fought against the rival Italian city of Genoa, was taken prisoner and dictated his memoires to a fellow prisoner while in captivity. The description of China and India by Marco Polo was one of the very first eyewitness reports reaching Europe after centuries. Ironically, it was not entirely believed, while we can say today that it was remarkably factual, with a few exceptions here and there.

Marco Polo visited Malabar, which he describes as "[t]he noblest and richest province of the world"[7] and the coast of Coromandel, where he notes that the local Brahmins were "the best and most honorable merchants that can be found. They can never be induced to lie, eat no flesh, drink no wine, and live with great austerity and in scrupulous honesty." This is no mean compliment, coming from another tradesman. He then pays homage to the wealth of the country, as his predecessors: "This king wears pearls and precious gems and jewels, worth an entire city." He then duly notes the contrast with the austerity of the life led by yogis and sadhus.

Beside geography and issues related to market and trade, Marco had a keen interest in religion. We find in *Il Milione* the story of Lord Buddha, related with clear sympathy, but with one substantial qualification: "Had he been baptized a Christian, he would certainly have become a great Saint."

In thirteenth century Europe, identity and religion went together and Christianity was the sole repository of truth. Gone were the days when an altar in Rome could celebrate the unknown god. The division was clear cut and the crusades only put this alternative in starker perspective: either with us or against us.

Even men of curiosity and goodwill such as Marco Polo, who felt sincere empathy with many of the peoples he met in his two decades of travel, could not venture beyond the pale. Marco Polo is simply saddened that the Revelation had not come to all and puzzled as to the reasons why it was so. Even greater intellectuals than Marco, such as Dante Alighieri, were not capable of going further than looking for exceptions and cut some corners in order to include in the salvation some of the most illustrious Roman (pagan) classical authors.

This is a new tint which colours chronicles and diaries from the Middle Ages onwards. While we have noted the similarities and recurrent themes common to the Graeco-Roman depiction of India, this is one new distinct feature.

In parallel, we assist to efforts at building bridges: the legend of St Thomas is one such. The story of St Thomas the evangelist, who reportedly came to India to spread the Gospel and died close to Chennai, is also included in the *Travels of Marco Polo*. It can be interpreted as a way to finding commonalities via the intercession of saints, a not so unusual solution in medieval Europe.

"Religions are not for separating men from one another, they are meant to bind them. It is a misfortune that today they are so distorted that they have become a potent cause of strife and mutual slaughter." This sentence of Mahatma Gandhi sounds true also when applied to past centuries.

AMBROSIO BEMBO

The tales of Marco Polo were instrumental in raising the attention of Europeans to 'the Indies'. In the late fifteenth century, Cristoforo Colombo, another Italian traveller, crossed the Atlantic and landed in America, in the belief of having arrived in the Indies. Early in the fifteenth century, the Portuguese decided to break the virtual monopoly of Venice over the Silk Route and put an end to the stranglehold of the Mamelukes in Egypt over the land routes to the East, by sailing round Africa. They did so successfully and landed in India, opening a new chapter in the relationship between India and Europe, not always happy, one must add.

While the Venetian merchants had been travelling in peace as private entrepreneurs, the new European adventurers were imbued with a spirit of conquest and would not refrain from military confrontation. This new spirit gives a different tone to diaries and chronicles of Europeans visiting the East.

The vantage point from Italy, however, remains commanding: Italians did not stop visiting India, but they were not the vanguard of hegemonic powers. They kept coming as they had before, as private individuals, out of curiosity or looking for personal gain and enrichment.

This is what makes many chronicles and diaries of Italian travellers to the East relevant today. Two of the most well known are Niccolo Manucci and Pietro della Valle.

Manucci ('a Samuel Pepys of Mogul India', as he was termed by the British) ran away from Venice in 1653, being 14; he came to India, where he tried his fortune as artilleryman at the service of Dara Shikoh, then as doctor and diplomatist; he died in Puducherry in 1717. His *Storia do Mogor*, written over a long span of time, in Portuguese, French and Italian, gives us a wealth of information and anecdotes over Mughal India and the civil war between Dara Shikoh and Aurangzeb. The perspective of Manucci is entirely personal. He likes Dara Shikoh and dislikes Aurangzeb out of pure personal inclinations. The English and Portuguese were jostling for national positions, but Manucci was his own man. In his memoires, one can feel the satisfaction of the self-made man: sometime sanctimonious but often acute and straight to the point in judging people or situations. As to the religious discourse, it is totally obstructed by prejudice: Manucci makes no exception. What we get from his *Storia* is the flavour of daily life in seventeenth century India: fashion, cooking, prejudices, passions. He has little analytical skills beyond his personal interest, but a good descriptive streak. The image of India emanating from his memoire is of a Land of Opportunity in the American sense: a land where a man can make his own fortune, based on his own skills. This is a new and additional layer, over the traditional strata we have already met: immensity of the geographical expanse, climatic excess, fabulous wealth, bizarre customs. This new feature will further expand under the Britishers: the East India Company would proffer the mirage of rapid wealth to all and everyone of its employees, all hoping to become 'nawabs' and return to show their riches at the promenade in Park Lane in London.

Another seventeenth century Italian traveller was the nobleman Pietro della Valle, from Rome, who visited India from 1623 to 1624. His letters were published, translated in various European languages and acquired notoriety for accuracy and precision. Contrary to Manucci, della Valle was an educated person, belonging to the elite. He travelled out of pure pleasure and diversion; a tourist in sum. He mingled with the Dutch, the English, the Portuguese and the Indian rulers, Hindu and Muslim alike. He felt equally at ease, basing his judgement on class distinction: his world view is seen through the prism of social classification. He had a scientific education too, and relished to use the compass, measuring degrees of latitude whenever possible. The same spirit he applied to his observations on India, precise and documented, if a bit pedantic. He combined pretensions to scientific exactitude with a vein of lunacy: he travelled trough India and all the way back to Italy with the embalmed body of his wife, who died in Persia, because he wanted her to rest in the church in Rome where he possessed his family tomb. His attention to detail was not matched by a talent for grasping the whole. The lack of empathy of della Valle with India and her culture can be taken as an example of the changing mood of the times: Europeans were no longer willing to learn and not even to be surprised; they would simply observe and judge. Again, this is particularly true for the religious discourse.

One notable exception to this general trend is, in my opinion, Ambrosio Bembo. In 1671, Ambrosio, a young gentleman of Venice, 19 years old, belonging to one of the most distinguished families in the city, decided to leave for the Orient:

> The desire to know is innate and natural to the spirit of mankind, whose special gift is the intellect, the sense that is always most eager to feed itself with knowledge. Many things are learned through theory, and more through practice. The world is a great book, which, when perused attentively, proffers teachings and delights with its variety.[8]

This is the incipit of Ambrosio's journal, never edited in his lifetime and published only in 1973. I find it remarkable; but what is even more interesting is that he actually maintained this approach during his long voyage, which brought him to Turkey, Syria, today's Iraq, Persia, Western India and back, over four years.

Bembo was already a war veteran, having fought in the campaign against the Ottomans in Candia. But at 19 he was still too young to enter full political life, in the Consiglio Grande, the Parliament of Venice. Unwilling to wait until his 25th anniversary with no specific business (since 'idleness eats away all virtue and is the worst companion for youth'), he decided to find a serious occupation in travelling. At that time, well before the 'Grand Tour' fashion, travelling was still mostly a practical need and a professional hazard. Not so for Bembo, or for della Valle before him, who travelled for leisure and instruction.

The chronicle of his experiences was written after his return, based on his travel notes (including the detailed budget of his journey), and accompanied by the illustrations of a French draughtsman, engaged by Bembo in Persia. It was left unpublished and forgotten until 1973 for reasons unknown.

Bembo in his journal refrains from any geopolitical consideration. Venice was losing her markets in the East while England, France and the Dutch were supplanting the Portuguese in India. Bembo simply describes the facts: the flourishing of the East India Company in Mumbai; the decay of the Portuguese establishments, suffocated by inertia and the ecclesiastical hold on civil power.

Young Bembo left Venice armed with the education of a nobleman of his times (he studied 'in the school of the Somaschi Fathers'): his intellectual frame of reference was based on Graeco-Roman antiquity. It served him extremely well, so much so that it makes one wonder whether our modern apparel is any better. The openness of mind of Bembo, his curiosity and acumen in discovering alien cultures and customs are truly remarkable. May be his young age helped, together with a clear mind, but Bembo is truly honest in his accounts: no cheap exoticism, no sanctimonious remarks. Bembo dislikes all forms of immoderate religious fervour and fanaticism. He duly pays respect to the prejudices of his times by describing all non-Christian beliefs as false (may be in order to make a possible censor happy, back in Europe); but then he notes revealingly that the Indians "make fun of our ceremonies as much as we do of theirs". In general terms, Bembo is a spirit of the Enlightenment *ante litteram*, curious of humanity in all its shades and forms, adopting an empiricist approach vis-à-vis mankind and the world. In a way, della Valle represents the old world, whose science is a revalidation of Aristotle, based on categories and hierarchy. Bembo's idea of science is very different: constant trial and error, in intellectual endeavours as much as in life. This gives Bembo much better insights into India and makes him today a very pleasant reading, where India and the East are immune from any orientalist contamination.

The issue of religious diversity was an open sore for most European travellers, who simply could not reconcile their view of the world with the reality of the extreme diversity of cults and beliefs in India. The best example of such disorientation that I could find is in the book of a celebrated French traveller, François Bernier, who travelled through India in 1656–1668. Bernier interrogated Indian wise men as to the plurality of creeds; this is the answer he got:

> We pretend not—they replied—that our law is of universal application. God intended it only for us, and this is the reason why we cannot receive a foreigner in our religion. We do not even say that yours is a false religion: it may be adapted to your wants and circumstances, God having no doubt, appointed very different ways of going to heaven.[9]

Such an answer was totally disconcerting to most Europeans in the seventeenth century. We have to wait for the Enlightenment to find the same equanimity (for instance, in Lessing's Nathan der Weise).

EMILIO SALGARI

Let me now to jump to the end of nineteenth century, beginning of twentieth century, a time of blind nationalism and imperialism in Europe, which brought destruction upon herself with the bloodbath of World War I. This was not an epoch for cross-cultural conversations. The image of the 'other' was by definition negative, in the absurd belief that only national self-assertion could serve the needs of modern times. With a few scholarly exceptions, most European literature, especially popular literature, on the Orient was the product of intellectual arrogance, coupled with prejudice. This is precisely the epoch of orientalism, as described by Edward Said.

However, in such a bleak picture, I am glad to recall the name of Emilio Salgari. Salgari was a humble practitioner in literature; he wrote feuilletons, paid by the line. He never ventured East beyond Venice and spent most of his life in Turin. What is remarkable about his books, adventure stories for boys, is that the hero of the narrative is not a European, but an Asian, a Malay pirate called Sandokan, unjustly deprived of his land by the Britishers. His adventures, together with his Indian friends, a Bengali and a Maharatha, are bound together by the struggle against the colonial power. Salgari's ethical assessment of the power of the British Empire is strongly negative. At the end of the best known of his books (*The Two Tigers*), set in India in 1857, this is the description he gives of the sack of Delhi by the Britishers: "The massacres in Delhi lasted for three days, horrible massacres that provoked the indignation not just of other European nations but even of England."[10] This sounds a fair assessment, but it was still uncommon at that time, when crimes in colonial wars were easily condoned.

In a cross-cultural conversation exercise, it is worth noting that generations of Italians, up to my generation, have received their first exposure to the idea of India through the novels of Salgari. An India described as an exotic setting (dangerous jungles, mysterious sects, wealthy maharajas, beautiful damsels); but also a country the young reader was invited to connect with and empathize, through the adventures of the hero.

I shall add that in 1976, an immensely popular television series based on Salgari was broadcast. The hero Sandokan was played by an Indian actor, Mr Kabir Bedi, who became instantly a household name, synonymous with daring and fairness. I can assure you this was all good publicity for India!

PIER PAOLO PASOLINI AND CARLO LEVI

It is now high time for me to conclude my chapter. I only want to add to the list of Italian travellers who shaped the image of India in my country two names belonging to twentieth century, Pier Paolo Pasolini and Carlo Levi.

They both were Leftist radicals, inclined to communism, even though with a peculiar humanitarian tinge. They travelled to India in 1960 and 1957, respectively, ready to pay homage to the land of antiquity and spirituality and also to the leading light of the non-aligned movement, an internationalist alternative to the American hegemonic model, as they saw it.

Pier Paolo Pasolini was a novelist and a film-maker, but above all a poet. He believed that the moral values of truth and justice were the domain of the poor and underprivileged; he also had strong opinions as to the decadence of mores in modern urban life; he longed for the supposed pristine purity and simplicity of village and country life. You will easily understand that this brought Pasolini to seek and see mostly poverty in India, in the slums of Mumbai and Kolkata. However, what makes his testimony relevant today, in the context of cross-cultural conversations, is Pasolini's sincerity of approach. He does not pretend to know and understand; he does not judge. He mostly feels, as poets are wont to do, and participates. No intellectual detachment for Pasolini: he wants to share, in a naïve and at times simplistic fashion, but also intriguingly sympathetic. This gives him some original glimpses, which strike as gems, in his book relating his travels to Mumbai, Delhi, Kolkata, Khajuraho, Kerala and Tamilnadu.

The first example I would like to offer is relevant to the feeling of disorientation I mentioned earlier, in the context of Christian European travellers to the Orient:

> It can seem absurd, but for the first time I realized that Catholicism does not comprise the whole world … I asked myself for the first time, in a strangely compelling manner, what fills this world, this subcontinent of 400 million souls. I had been for too short a time in India to find a replacement to my idea of State religion: religious freedom was a sort of a wide chasm opening in front of me, giving me the shivers from vertigo. Only little by little could I get used to this condition of free religious choice, which on the one hand gives the sense of a sort of superfluity of any religion, but on the other hand is so rich of religious spirit.[11]

I regard this paragraph as a fitting tribute to the spirituality of India by a man who sought in religion not just liberation but fraternity and justice. The puzzlement of Pasolini, overcome with awe when faced with the diversity of the divine, is transformed into abandon to the free flow of religious inspirations, in its thousand avatars.

The same sentiment of quasi-mystic participation is to be found in the final sentence of Pasolini's book, in a night illuminated by the funeral pyres, along the ghats on the Ganges, in Benares: "Never, in no place and in no time of our Indian stay, did we ever feel such a profound sense of communion, peace and, almost joy."[12]

Coming from a man who resented death as the ultimate injustice, this is a moving reflection on India's capacity to integrate death within life.

Pasolini was no doubt sincere, but the 1960s were also the time of the 'hippy generation' enamourment with India, seen as the land of enlightenment and liberation. The image of India was intertwined with the beat generation protest at the alleged lack of genuineness of Western lifestyles. In their quest for the sources of truth, youngsters came in droves to India, seeking new paths to salvation.

This fashion made unlikely victims. Carlo Levi, a writer but also a doctor, was an eminently practical person. His travel journal is the depiction of India as a country struggling with the challenges of development, in 1957. Levi admires Nehru and traces of him a very flattering portrait, as a man of power but also capable of compassion; a man of action but also an intellectual.

Nevertheless, even as sober a writer as Levi falls under the spell of mysterious India: "... India appears to open to us—not in the form of ideas, fantasies or feelings, but rather as living realities, faces, figures and persons—the spectacle of our century's old story."[13] Levi reads in the India of 1957 the marks of the past in Europe, the ghosts of classical antiquity. And in the wake of his return to Italy, he observes: "I don't feel as if I am returning from another world, but rather from an inner world."[14]

It might sound a bit of a cliché but it is also true: India makes most European visitors, and Italians are no exceptions, feel as if they were faced with a land of deep emotion, of fertile human experience.

This sentiment of Levi is shared by many. It can be productive when applied, with humility, to the better understanding of a different culture. It can also lead to annoying stereotypical simplifications. India is a good teacher for those who want to listen. But it chooses her own disciples and let the others go convinced to have understood all, while profoundly ignorant.

The moon of the Indian sky is different from the moon in the northern hemisphere. As Levi wrote: "The reclining, contemplative moon of this sky makes one think of the stability of a pendulum, compromise, tolerance, and harmony."[15]

These features—compromise, tolerance, harmony—are also part and parcel of the image of India as perceived by foreign travellers. Not the only ones, but certainly the most endearing and befitting to conclude this brief survey.

NOTES AND REFERENCES

1. Curzio Rufo, *Storie di Alessandro Magno* (BUR, Milano: 2005), 886.
2. Curzio Rufo, *Storie di Alessandro Magno*, 891.
3. Curzio Rufo, *Storie di Alessandro Magno*, 893.
4. Curtius, citato, *Storie di Alessandro Magno*, 894.
5. Arriano, *Storia di Alessandro*, Libro VII (Milano: Rusconi, 1980), 380.
6. Curtius, *Storie di Alessandro Magno*, 897.
7. Marco Polo, *Il Libro Di Marco Polo Detto Il Milione, Nella Versione Trecentesca Dell'ottimo* (Torino: Einaudi, 1982), 175.
8. Ambrosio Bembo, *The Travels and Journal of Ambrosio Bembo* (Berkeley, California: University of California Press, 2007).
9. Francois Bernier, *Travels in the Mogul Empire (1656-1668)* (New Delhi: Asian Educational Services, 2010), 328.
10. *Emilio Salgari, Le Due Tigri* (Torino), 246.
11. Pier Paolo Pasolini, L'odore dell'India (1961), Guanda, Parma 2003.

    Per la prima volta, potra' sembrare assurdo, ho avuto l'impressione che il cattolicesimo non coincida con il mondo: ma la separazione delle due entita' e' stata cosi' inaspettata e violenta, da costituire una specie di trauma…Mi sono chiesto allora, per la prima volta in maniera urgente, da che cosa fosse riempito questo mondo, questo subcontinente di quattrocento milioni di anime. Era troppo poco tempo che mi trovavo in India, per trovare qualcosa da sostituire alla mia religione di stato: la liberta' religiosa era una specie di vuoto a cui mi affacciavo con le vertigini. Solo un po' alla volta mi sarei abituato a questa condizicne di libera scelta religiosa, che se da una parte da' un senso come di gratuita' di ogni religione, dall'altra e' cosi' ricca di spirito religioso. (p. 24)

12. Pasolini, citato, "Mai in nessun posto, in nessun'ora, in nessun atto, di tutto il nostro soggiorno indiano, abbiamo provato un cosi' profondo senso di comunione, di tranquillita' e, quasi, di gioia" (p. 110).
13. Carlo Levi, *Essays on India (1957)* (London: Hesperus, 2007), 5.
14. Levi, *Essays on India*, 79.
15. Levi, *Essays on India*, 7.

About the Editor and Contributors

CROSS CULTURAL CONVERSATION

The CCC conferences aim at exploring the contending visions and choices that are before us today. Based on the recognition of a call for human solidarity as a powerful rhetoric in national and international contexts, these conferences seek to bring about changes in the present environment, drawing on the perception that respect for cultural diversity demands a more complex understanding of what a pluralistic society really entails. Indeed, there are many voices that express this common human aspiration for achieving solidarity in all its various facets—social, ethical, religious, economic and political. The modes of persuasions are diverse, as is to be expected. Approaches and preferences may be secular or religious, philosophical strategies can be of various genres (essentialistic, pragmatic or otherwise) just as suggestions for practical, political implementations may also vary.

The participants of this open conversation attempt to closely examine a range issues and concerns with the hope that the very richness of the interactions and exchanges will make us all aware of various asymmetries that are there in different contexts. This in turn will gradually help us to envision—through repeated cross-cultural conversation—how to build those bridges that are lacking at present. The endeavour here is to provide a positive ambience where it is possible to diagnose in collaboration those collective prejudices that act as a divisive force, how these are actually perpetuated in and through theoretical discourse affecting negatively practical policymaking. On the other hand, the aim is to unlearn these prejudices while projecting visions for the future in the name of human solidarity.

THE EDITOR

Anindita N. Balslev is a philosopher based in India and Denmark. Her educational and professional experience in India, France, USA and Denmark has inspired her to create a forum for 'Cross-cultural Conversation' (CCC). The international CCC conferences that she organizes have lead to thought-provoking discussions and publications. 'On India: Self-image and Counter-image' was the theme of the conference that she organized in 2010 with the support of IGNCA and ICCR, New Delhi.

She has served on the boards of several important international organizations/societies and is a founding member of the International Society for Science and Religion.

She has published many essays in professional journals in the areas of philosophy, religion and culture. She is the author of several books. To mention a few: A *Study of Time in Indian Philosophy* (Delhi, 3rd edition, 2009), *Cultural Otherness: Correspondence with Richard Rorty* (USA, 2nd edition, 2000), *Indian Conceptual World* (2012), *The Enigma of I-consciousness* (Delhi, 2013). She is also the editor of the volume entitled *Cross-cultural Conversation* (cultural criticism series, AAR, USA, 1996) and the co-editor of the volumes entitled *Religion and Time* (The Netherlands, 1993) and of *Compassion in the World's Religions* (Berlin, 2010).

THE CONTRIBUTORS

Ugo Astuto has a long career as an Italian diplomat. He was Deputy Head of Mission and Minister Counsellor at Italian Embassy in India at the time of this conference. He is also an avid orientalist with a keen interest in travelogues and in Indian literature.

Lokesh Chandra is a renowned scholar of Tibetan, Mongolian and Sino-Japanese Buddhism and of Buddhist iconography. He is currently Director, International Academy of Indian Culture, and has also served as Vice-President of the Indian Council for Cultural Relations and Chairman of the Indian Council of Historical Research. He has to his credit 581 works and edited texts.

Johan Galtung is a prominent Norwegian sociologist and founder of the discipline of peace and conflict studies. He is also a member of the Norwegian Academy of Science and Letters. His dedication to peace has been recognized with 10 honorary doctorates and an Alternative Nobel Prize. He has published 140 books and 1500 articles.

Galtung is the author of a number of books. His classic autobiography, his correspondence with Nehru, Jammu and Kashmir (1949–1964), and his essays on Hinduism have been widely acclaimed. He has travelled and lectured through five continents and has been very supportive of the CCC international conferences.

D.R. Kaarthikeyan is at present a legal advisor (Human Rights and Responsibilities—Corporate Affairs). He has formerly served as the Director General of Central Reserve Police Force, and Director of the Central Bureau of Investigation of India. Karthikeyan was awarded the Padma Shri in 2010 for his contribution to the field of Indian Civil Service. He is the President of *Life Positive* magazine.

Kapil Kapoor is the Rector at Jawaharlal Nehru University and Professor of English and Concurrent Professor of Sanskrit Studies, New Delhi. He is an eminent scholar with several publications to his credit such as 'Literary Theory: Indian Conceptual Framework' and 'Dimensions of Panini Grammar'.

N. Kazanas is the Director of Omilos Meleton in Athens, Greece. He is the author of *Indo-Aryan Origins and other Vedic Issues* (Delhi, 2009).

Madhu Purnima Kishwar is a well-known feminist and the Senior Fellow at the Centre for the Study of Developing Societies (CSDS), based in Delhi. She is the Founder President of the Manushi Sangathan. She is the Convener of a series of international conferences on 'Religions and Cultures in the Indic Civilization' and has authored and edited several books.

Sukrita Paul Kumar is a writer and poet, researching and teaching literature. An Honorary Fellow of International Writing Programme, University of Iowa (USA) and a former Fellow of the Indian Institute of Advanced Study, Shimla, she was also an invited poet in residence at Hong Kong Baptist University. She has several publications to her credit.

Ashish Nandy is a leading Indian political psychologist, a social theorist and a contemporary cultural and political critic. He was Senior Fellow and Director of the Centre for the Study of Developing Societies (CSDS) for several years. He has many publications to his credit such as *The Intimate Enemy*, *Alternative Sciences*, *Traditions, Tyranny and Utopias and Others*.

Dietmar Rothermund is Professor Emeritus, Heidelberg, and a promising name in the field of cross-cultural studies, with several journal articles to his credit. He is the author of such acclaimed books as *An Economic History of India* (2nd edition, 1993), *India: The Rise of an Asian Giant* (2008), and the co-author of *A History of India* (4th revised edition, 2004).

Shyam Saran was former Foreign Secretary in the Government of India during 2004–2006. He served as Prime Minister's Special Envoy for Indo-US civil nuclear issues. In 2011, he was honoured with a Padma Bhushan by the government for his sustained contribution to public life and instilling social conscience.

Balmiki Prasad Singh is the present Governor of Sikkim, India, apart from being a distinguished scholar, thinker and public servant. He has several publications.

Index